MICHELIN

PRAGUE

—in your pocket—

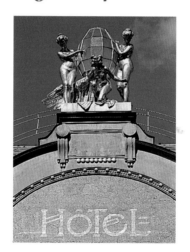

HOTEL

PHOTOGRAPH CREDITS
Pavel Štecha title page, 5, 6, 9, 11, 12, 15, 16, 17, 23, 24,
25, 27, 28, 29, 30 (top, bottom), 31, 32, 33, 38, 39, 40,
42, 43, 44, 45, 46, 47, 49, 50, 51 (left, right), 53, 54, 55,
56, 58, 59, 61, 62, 65, 66, 67, 68, 71 (top, bottom), 73,
74, 75, 76, 77, 81 (top, bottom), 82, 83, 84, 85, 87, 88,
89, 91, 92, 96, 97, 99, 101, 104; The Travel Library front
cover, back cover, 19, 21, 34, 37, 106, 108, 111, 116, 119;
The Travel Library/ David Forman 125; The Travel
Library/G Walden 107; BFI Stills, Posters and Designs
79.

*Front cover: Týn Church; back cover: Charles Bridge at dawn;
title page: detail of Evropa Hotel*

MANUFACTURE FRANÇAISE DES PNEUMATIQUES MICHELIN

Société en commandite par actions au capital de 2 000 000 000 de francs

Place des Carmes-Déchaux – 63 Clermont-Ferrand (France)

R.C.S. Clermont-Fd 855 200 507

© Michelin et Cie. Propriétaires-Éditeurs 1996

Dépôt légal Avril 96 – ISBN 2-06-650501-3 – ISSN en cours

Printed in the EU 3-96

CONTENTS

INTRODUCTION

Prague is an enchanted city, a magical place where 1 000 years of history casts a potent spell over inhabitants and visitors alike. The 'city of a hundred spires' miraculously escaped destruction in the Second World War, leaving an impossible, almost surreal treasure hoard of Romanesque, Gothic, Baroque, Art Nouveau and cubist architecture.

Surrealism – the art of dreams – is a recurring theme in Prague. This was, after all, the city where defenestration – the ill-tempered throwing of people out of windows – was the preferred form of punishment. Some of Prague's dreams have been happier than others: the Golem – an unruly monster created by Rabbi Löw – was cheerful enough, if a little hyperactive. But this was also the city where writer Franz Kafka recorded his claustrophobic, tortured visions: 'Prague does not let go ... this little mother has claws.'

The creative imagination has always flourished in Prague, nowhere more joyfully than in music 'the heart of the Czechs'. Smetana, Dvořák, Janáček and Martinů all rose to prominence in the city, and Mozart chose it for the première of *Don Giovanni*.

The Prague Spring Music Festival, held in May and June each year, gives visitors an opportunity to glimpse the elusive spirit of the place. Or you can climb to the castle and look out over the 'Golden City', largely untouched by war, untroubled by obtrusive modern development, its copper cupolas turned green with age. In winter the view is even more magical: no city wears its mantle of snow more beautifully than Prague,

The Vltava river regularly flooded in the past, and despite a series of dams upstream in the 20C there is concern it may flood again.

recalling the Good King Wenceslas of the 19C Christmas carol.

Other visitors may prefer to search for the spirit of Prague in the timeless atmosphere of the taverns which have changed little since the Good Soldier Švejk – the national anti-hero created by Jaroslav Hašek – drank there.

HOW TO USE THIS GUIDE

This guide is divided into four main
sections:

Background sets the scene, beginning with a
summary of Prague's colourful and often
turbulent history, outlining the people and
events which have shaped her development,
and the heroes and legends of the past.

*Prague Castle,
romantically
sihouetted against
the evening sky.*

There are also special features on the Czech composers and writers who have contributed to the rich cultural and artistic heritage of the city.

Exploring Prague opens with a list of the top ten sights you should try to see on your visit to Prague. There are then six detailed itineraries, specially designed to help you explore the key sights and attractions within the different areas of the city. They cover the Royal Route, Prague Castle and Hradčany, the Little Quarter (Malá Strana), the Old Town (Staré Město), the Jewish Town (Josefov) and the Golden Cross. There are special features on The Golem and Music in Prague. A section on Museums and Galleries lists not only the main attractions, but many smaller ones as well, together with opening hours. The section is rounded off by suggestions for whole and half-day excursions that can be made from Prague.

Enjoying Your Visit provides friendly, no-nonsense advice on the day-to-day holiday activities which can make the difference between a good holiday and a great one – eating out, shopping, entertainment and nightlife, and details of the main events in Prague as well as the all-important factor – the weather.

A-Z Factfinder is an easy-to-use reference section packed with useful information, covering everything you may need to know on your visit, from tipping to transport, or from using the telephone to tourist information offices.

A word of warning: opening hours and telephone numbers are subject to alteration, so be sure to double check first.

HISTORY

A City of Legend

Prague lies at the very heart of Europe. In a famous utterance Bismarck asserted that, 'He who holds Bohemia, holds Europe.' It is not surprising, then, that the lands surrounding what is now Prague have been fought over throughout history. In the 5C BC the Celtic **Boii** (who gave their name to Bohemia) were displaced by Germanic tribes who later made a nuisance of themselves to the Roman Empire, secure in the knowledge that the River Danube separated them from the all-conquering legions. With the fall of Rome in the 5C, the **Huns** moved into the area, to be supplanted in their turn by the warlike **Avars** a century later.

Around the 6C the first **Slavs** (ancestors of the Czechs) established themselves. According to legend, it was during this period that the city of Prague was founded. **Princess Libuše**, daughter of the improbably named King Crocus, was noted for her abilities as a prophetess. One day Libuše had a visitation of a 'town whose glory will one day reach the stars'. At the precise spot described by the prophetess (Vyšehrad, *see* p.96) her courtiers discovered a man putting the finishing touches to his cottage by fixing a doorstep – '*práh*' in Czech. Building of the new city of Praha began immediately.

It is a feature of Prague that practically every aspect of its history and building has been explained by a legend, which is often preferable to the plain facts. However, since the 9C legend has had to compete with reliable history. At this time the Slav ruler of Bohemia, **Prince Bořivoj**, was converted to

Christianity by the Greek missionaries
Methodius and Cyril.

Bořivoj's grandson – the first of many
royal **Wenceslases** (*Václav* in Czech) – built
the first church dedicated to St Vitus at
Prague Castle. He also strengthened Prague
strategically by building the castle at
Vyšehrad on the right bank of the Vltava
river. For his trouble, the Christian
Wenceslas was murdered by his pagan
brother, **Boleslav the Cruel**.

Despite Boleslav's shortcomings as a
brother, he proved an effective ruler and
consolidated Přemyslid power. The martyred
Wenceslas's compensation was that he
became the patron saint of Bohemia,
immortalized in a popular Christmas carol.

A Centre of Trade

Romanesque Prague was a rapidly
expanding commercial centre, well placed
on the European trade routes, with a good
river crossing. Churches and convents were
built with profits made in the thriving
market on Staroměstské náměstí. In 973, in
the reign of **Boleslav the Pious**, Prague
became a bishopric. Significantly, this new
bishop was controlled by the archbishop of
Mainz which marked the beginning of
German influence in Bohemia; over the
next century German merchants from the
Holy Roman Empire took an increasing
interest in Prague and Bohemia.

In the 12C the first stone bridge across the
Vltava was built and named after the king's
consort, Judith. This facilitated further
building and fortification on both banks of
the river. In 1257 the most remarkable of all
the Přemyslid kings, **Přemysl Otakar II**,
founded the Malá Strana (Little Quarter) to

*Statue of St
Wenceslas, who
ruled Prague from
921–35, when he
was murdered by
order of his brother,
Boleslav.*

accommodate the German merchants who had flooded into Prague. This influx was treated with great suspicion by the Bohemian aristocracy. But Přemysl Otakar, who had built a kingdom which stretched from the Adriatic to the Baltic, had his own way of settling the German issue – by attempting to seize the throne of the Holy Roman Empire for himself. He failed, and was forced to surrender to Rudolf von Habsburg, who had his own dynastic aspirations. The death throes of the Přemyslid line were bloody even by the standards of the day. But despite these murderous royal squabbles, Prague flourished economically. Eventually, an exasperated nobility, no doubt prompted by merchants desperate for stability, offered the throne to **John of Luxemburg**.

John's reign was not a success; he treated Europe like one vast tournament and finally, old and blind and tied between two Czech knights, this quixotic Francophile died fighting the English at Crécy. However his son, another Wenceslas who decided to change his name to Charles, was to preside over Prague's first Golden Age.

The ceilings of the New Lands Rolls rooms of the Royal Palace are decorated with the crests of clerks who worked there from the 16C to 18C.

Prague's Golden Age

King **Charles I** (and from 1355 the Holy Roman Emperor Charles IV) made Prague his imperial capital and one of the most important cities in Europe.

Charles also brought the Gothic style to Prague. During his reign the university was founded, he built the Charles Bridge, St Vitus Cathedral, monasteries, churches, and even a New Town (Nové Město) to accomodate the host of newly arrived students, clerics, artists and merchants.

Under Charles, the Czech language and Czech culture flourished and Prague was made an archbishopric answerable only to Rome.

Golden Ages tend to be followed by less happy periods, however. **Wenceslas IV** lacked the diplomatic skills of his father, Charles the Great, although, in fairness, it is unlikely that any king could have steered a trouble-free course through the religious disturbances of the early 15C which were finally to erupt in the Reformation a century and a half later, tearing Europe apart.

A scene from an early illustrated manuscript.

Religious Upheaval

In Bohemia, religious differences were exacerbated by the old tensions between the Czech and German population, and by strains in the Feudal system. Nationalists made **Jan Hus**, the first Czech rector of the Charles University, their unlikely figurehead after he had railed against the abuses of the Church and been burned at the stake for his trouble. In subsequent riots the first of Prague's notorious defenestrations occurred, in which Hussites flung three Catholic councillors and seven unfortunate burghers from windows high up in the Nové Město Town Hall.

A century of religious and political turmoil ensued until, in 1526, the first of the **Habsburg dynasty** – who were to rule Bohemia until 1918 – ascended the throne. Improbably, since the new dynasty were Catholic kings in a country with a taste for nationalism and Protestantism, the Habsburgs consolidated their position. The reign of the third emperor, **Rudolf II** (1576–1611), saw the blossoming of Prague's second Golden Age.

The nobles and burghers of Prague offered to settle Rudolf's debts and rebuild the castle if he moved the imperial court from Vienna – then threatened by the Turks. Rudolf was mad but he was not foolish. For the first time in two centuries, Prague became the imperial capital and it flourished.

An Imperial Capital

A passionate patron of the arts and an inquisitive intellectual, Rudolf filled his capital with painters, sculptors, astronomers and alchemists. Prague became a hive of creative activity: a fantastic city presided over by a sad, mad king obsessed with finding the Elixir of Life and the Philosopher's Stone.

But the shadow following Prague's second Golden Age was even darker than before. In 1618 Europe plunged into the **Thirty Years' War**. The same year saw Prague's second defenestration: reason, tolerance and two governors of Bohemia and their secretary flew out of the window.

The 'Winter King', **Frederick of the Palatinate**, proved a poor champion of the Protestant cause and was forced to flee Prague after a disastrous defeat at the Battle of the White Mountain, in 1620. The victors reconverted Prague to Catholicism with a vengeance. On the anniversary of the event 27 Protestant leaders were executed, three commoners hanged in Staroměstské náměstí and 150 000 Protestants exiled. A positive aspect of an unhappy period was the importation of the baroque style by the Jesuits, who organized the **Counter Reformation**: Italian architects and their pupils filled the city with palaces, churches and convents.

By the 18C, Prague had become a quiet provincial town. Quiet, that is, when the armies of Bavaria, Saxony and France were not attacking it during the **War of Austrian Succession** (1740–48) or the Prussians during the **Seven Years' War**. But by now Prague was a pawn. All vestiges of Bohemian independence had been stripped away, the Czech language was suppressed and Vienna was firmly established as the seat of power.

The Czech Revival

In the early 19C came the first stirrings of national revival. Three generations of

A panoramic view across Prague, with the Little Quarter Square in the foreground and the Vltava river in the distance.

writers, historians and philologists laboured tirelessly to codify the Czech language, and visitors to Prague can still find monuments to Dobrovský, Jungmann, Mácha and Palacký, erected by a grateful nation. As the Habsburg Empire slowly died, the Czech nation came to life. The iron grip of the old Austrian Chancellor **Prince Metternich** loosened while Czech industrialization and nationalism strengthened. Towards the close of the century, Czech aspirations found new voice in the music of Dvořák, Smetana and later in Janáček. Czechs also won concessions in language laws, although German remained the official language.

On 28 October 1918 the Republic of Czechoslovakia was proclaimed, with **Tomáš Masaryk** as its first president. Prague became the natural capital of the new state, and enjoyed 20 years of glorious independence. It was a frenetic, creative time: the city became a magnet for the avant garde, its café society bustling with writers, artists, architects and musicians.

After the sunshine came the night. It was a long, dark night, full of terrible dreams: the Munich Agreement; the Reich Protectorate; the Second World War; Heydrich; the

A fine example of Art Nouveau can be seen in this entrance hall and doorway.

Václav Havel was unanimously elected President by the Federal Assembly on 29 December 1989, following the Velvet Revolution.

Holocaust, and after the Germans, the Red Army. Under Stalinism, Prague slept uneasily behind closed blinds. There was the false dawn in 1968, 'socialism with a human face', until the hopes and reforms known as the **Prague Spring** were crushed by invading Wasraw Pact forces. Twenty years of bleak 'normalisation' followed. Then came the real dawn with the collapse of the communist system worldwide and the remarkable and peaceful **Velvet Revolution** of 1989. Sadly, inevitably perhaps, Slovakia then chose separation and a new **Czech Republic** was born.

Prague, as beautiful as ever, is like a sleeping princess in a Bohemian fairytale startled to find herself awake, shocked by the world she finds herself in. But Prague will cope, as she always has, and will occupy her rightful place at the heart of Europe.

Great Czech Composers

Bedřich Smetana (1824–84) was the son of a brewer in Eastern Bohemia. After studying music in Prague, he taught at a school in Staroměstské náměstí and later spent some time as a conductor and teacher in Göteborg in Sweden. Smetana wrote several symphonic poems, the Czech national opera *The Bartered Bride* and three other operas, when in 1874 he suddenly became deaf. In spite of that, he went on to compose *My Country*, a set of six symphonic poems, among which *Vltava* is perhaps his most famous piece, the string quartet *From My Life* and other operas such as *Libuše* (*see* p.86).

Antonín Dvořák (1841–1904) was the son of an innkeeper and butcher in a small town near Prague. After studying for three years at the Prague Organ School he played viola in the opera orchestra and wrote his first compositions. In 1884 Dvořák made the first of several visits to London. From 1892 until 1895 he was director of the National Conservatory of Music in New York, which gave him the inspiration for his magnificent *New World* symphony. His *Cello Concerto* and opera *Rusalka* (*Water nymph*), as well as his religious music – *Te Deum* and *Stabat Mater* – are internationally popular.

Leoš Janáček (1854–1928) was born in Moravia. He studied at the Prague Organ School and later became professor of the Prague Conservatory. Janáček's best-known works are his operas *Jenufa*, the *Makropoulos Case* and *The Cunning Little Vixen*, but he also wrote many chamber and piano pieces.

Bohuslav Martinů (1890–1959) studied first in Prague and then in Paris, where he lived until the war. He then spent his life in the USA, France and Switzerland where he died. Martinů combined modern music with Czech folk melodies. He wrote several operas (*Julietta*, *The Marriage*, and *The Greek*

Passion), as well as ballet,
symphonic and chamber
music.

The Dvořák Museum in winter.

Czech Writers

Švejk – the unpeturbed, matter-of-fact hero of **Jaroslav Hašek**'s (1883–1923) comic novel *The Good Soldier Švejk* – is considered by some Czechs to embody certain national characteristics. The Good Soldier's obtuse behaviour leads his superiors in the army of the Austro-Hungarian Empire to consider him a hopeless idiot. But is he? Švejk disobeys orders, avoids work he doesn't want to do, enjoys himself and pokes fun at authority – and all with impunity.

The contemporary Czech writer Milan Kundera recalls that on one occasion the Communist First Secretary Gustav Husák had to cancel a speech to students because

Illustration from The Good Soldier Švejk, by Jaroslav Hašek.

This plaque commemorating Franz Kafka is situated on the site of the house where he was born, on Kaprová street.

they would not stop chanting: 'Long live the Communist Party! Long live Husák!' The incident was pure Švejk.

Milan Kundera (1929–), who now lives in France, sheds light on a different aspect of the Czech psyche. *The Unbearable Lightness of Being* is a beautifully written novel: by turns moving and philosophical, erotic and intellectual, with flashes of highly original insight.

Kundera's *The Book of Laughter and Forgetting*, is semi-autobiographical.

Karel Čapek (1890–1938), whose science fiction gave us the word 'robot', writes wonderfully of Prague in *Intimate Things*.

Those with a taste for the exotic should try to find the story *Le passant de Prague* or *The Wandering Jew* by **Guillaume Apollinaire** (1880–1918).

Arguably the most important writer who came from and wrote about Prague was **Franz Kafka** (1883–1924). Typifying the cultural and linguistic richness that the city once enjoyed, he was a Jew who could read Czech but wrote in German. It has to be said that his dark, claustrophobic novels and short stories tinged with paranoia are not everybody's idea of holiday reading. But Prague is there, like a recurring character, in all his work.

A happier face of the Prague Jewish tradition is shown by **Ivan Klíma** (1931–), who confronts even nightmares with wry humour. Look for *My Golden Trades*.

EXPLORING PRAGUE

MUST SEE

The city of Prague is such a treasure house that it is extremely difficult to select the top ten attractions. However, the following are not only essential Prague experiences, they have been carefully chosen so that visitors using the guide will make further discoveries of their own, and leave this magical city with a rich store of unforgettable memories.

The Charles Bridge
Jewish Cemetery and 'Old-New' Synagogue
Historic Wenceslas Square
Music – in concert halls and churches
Old Town Square
Art Nouveau (Municipal House and Evropa Hotel)
The Castle and St Vitus's Cathedral
St Nicholas's Church (Malá Strana)
Shopping for Bohemian crystal

The Municipal House is one of Prague's most splendid Art Nouveau buildings.

THE ROYAL ROUTE

From the metro station Náměstí Republiky – Powder Tower (Prašná brána) – Celetná street – Old Town Square (Staroměstské náměstí) – Little Square (Malé náměstí) – Karlova street – Charles Bridge (Karlův Most) – Mostecká street – Malostranské náměstí – Nerudova street – to Prague Castle (Pražský hrad)

Also known as **The Coronation Way**, this walk includes many of Prague's most interesting historical buildings. It is a long walk, with a steep climb at the end, and there is so much to see and enjoy that visitors can easily spend half a day – or even a day – completing it.

The walk begins at the place where the kings of Bohemia lived in the 15C to be nearer to the bustling life of the city than they were at Prague Castle. Today, the site of the palace is occupied by the **Municipal House** (Obecní dům), on the Square of the

One of the figures adorning the Powder Tower which were added in 1875 during restoration work.

Republic (Náměstí Republiky). Unfortunately, nothing remains of the huge medieval building, only the name of a street – Kings Court Street (Králodvorská).

On leaving the **Náměstí Republiky** metro station, the Municipal House is the large, richly decorated building on the west side of the square. Built in the Art Nouveau style between 1905 and 1911, it was intended as a centre of cultural and social life in Prague. Concerts and balls are still held in its main hall, named after the Czech composer Smetana. Generations of boys and girls have attended dance courses in the smaller salons of the Municipal House. In the **Sal Primátorský** (Mayor's Salon) there are allegorical paintings by Alfons Mucha. There is also a restaurant and a café on the ground floor.

In days gone by, coronation processions entered the Staré Město by the medieval **Powder Tower** (Prašná brána). Originally the eastern town gate, it was built in the 1470s to replace an older one. Its architect, Benedikt Ried, decorated the gate richly as it was in the vicinity of the Royal Palace. The tower is so-called because gun powder was stored there in the 17C; you can still see the tower on the left side of the Municipal House. Walk through it, and follow the street U Prašné brány, which soon becomes Celetná street. But before entering Celetná, turn left to see the spacious **fruit market** (Ovocný trh) in front of the **Estates Theatre** (Stavovské divadlo) which Mozart chose for the première of his opera *Don Giovanni*.

Return to Celetná street (its name comes from '*calta*', a kind of bread roll made by the bakers who once had their shops here). On your left, at the corner of Celetná and

Ovocný trh, you will see Prague's most famous cubist house: **House at the Black Madonna** (U Černé Matky Boží). A medieval statue on the corner gave the house its evocative name.

On the right-hand side of the street, among the other baroque buildings, look out for the **Manhart Palace** with its theatre and, further on, the blue-and-white **Caretto-Millesimo Palace**. This once housed the Institute of Marxism-Leninism – today it is part of the university. On the left-hand side, practically at Staroměstské náměstí (the Old Town Square), is the **Sixt House** with the café **U Sixtů**. Next door to the Sixt House is

The Gothic façade of Týn Church is dominated by the steeples and the gold effigy of the Virgin Mary.

a neo-Renaissance building where you can
see paintings by one of the most popular
Czech painters, Mikoláš Aleš, depicting St
Wenceslas as a knight, and the Three Magi.

Now we are on **Staroměstské náměstí**, the
Old Town Square, which has seen 1 000
years of history, including celebrations and
burnings, royal pageants and royal
executions. In the Middle Ages, this was the
central marketplace, with the customs office
(*Ungelt*) and the main town church – **Týn
Church** or the **Church of Our Lady Before
Týn** (Kostel Panny Marie před Týnem). With
its irregular and strangely disturbing spires,
it's like something from the Brothers Grimm.
The construction of this magnificent
building started in the second half of the
14C at the place where, centuries before, a
chapel used by merchants selling their
goods had stood. The Gothic church with its
distinctive spires was finished much later, in
the 15C, under the 'Hussite' King George of
Poděbrady. On the main façade there was a
statue of the king holding a golden chalice –
the emblem of the Hussites – but after the
Battle of the White Mountain the statue was
melted down to make the present one of the
Virgin Mary, the gold of the chalice being
used for her aureole. To get into the church
on the east side of the square, go through
the houses of what were once **Týn School**.

Across narrow Týnská street, on the left
side of the church, there is the recently
restored **House of the Stone Bell** (Dům u
kamenného zvonu), the oldest complete
Gothic house in the city. Further on you
cannot miss the strawberries-and-cream
façade of the late baroque (rococo) **Golz-
Kinský Palace** (palác Goltz-Kinských) which
houses temporary collections of the

*The Golz-Kinský
Palace, on the Old
Town Square, is an
extraordinary
rococo confection.*

National Gallery and a good music shop on the ground floor. Franz Kafka's readers will be interested to know that his father used to have his shop in this building. In February 1948, Klement Gottwald, later the first Communist President of the Czechoslovak Republic, addressed the people of Prague from the balcony to announce what he called the 'victory of the working class' and what historians now call a *coup d'état*.

In the middle of the square is the Art Nouveau monument to Master Jan Hus by Ladislav Šaloun. This was unveiled in 1915 to celebrate the 500th anniversary of the

reformer's death at the stake (*see* p.13). There used to be another sculpture in the square, a baroque column supporting the Virgin Mary. This was destroyed by the crowd who came to the square to celebrate the end of the First World War and the end of Habsburg rule. The Catholic Church was so closely identified with the Habsburg dynasty in the popular imagination that the Virgin bore the brunt of their wrath.

Another important building in the square is the **Old Town Hall** (Staroměstská radnice). For the energetic, there is a beautiful view of the city from the tower. The **Astronomical Clock** dates from the beginning of the 15C and shows not only the time but also the astronomical calendar. There are four mechanical figures which move every hour: the Turk with a mandolin; the Rich Man with a money bag and Vanity with a mirror. All are shaking their heads

The massive Jan Hus monument, in Old Town Square, bears the inscription 'pravda vítězí' – Truth Prevails.

and saying 'no' to Death, who replies 'yes' and opens his mouth to call them from this world. Meanwhile, the 12 apostles and Jesus parade in two small windows above the clock. At the end of the performance a cock crows. The lowest part of the clock is a one-year calendar with 12 paintings representing each month of the year and the 12 signs of the zodiac.

As with many things in Prague, there is a legend concerning the clock. It is said that when it was completed its maker, Master Hanuš, was blinded with a red-hot poker by the burghers to ensure that he did not repeat his work for any other city. Today, more cheerful civic duties are conducted behind the Renaissance window on the first floor of the Town Hall. This is the wedding hall where smart Prague weddings are held. The distinctive house, decorated with black-and-white Renaissance *sgraffito,* is called

The lower portion of the Astronomical Clock on the Old Town Hall displays the months of the year.

Distinctive black and white sgraffito decorates the House of the Minute, part of the Old Town Hall.

House of the Minute (Dům U minuty): it forms part of the Town Hall. Today the square has become a market once more, with stalls where craftsmen such as blacksmiths and potters sell their goods.

When it is time to leave the square, walk

Matthias Braun's splendid statues support the portals of the Clam-Gallas Palace.

past the Old Town Hall into Malé náměstí
(Small Square) with its iron fountain grille,
old pharmacy and the famous ironmonger's
shop, U Rotta. Just past the Mappin and
Webb shop, turn right into Karlova ulice
(Charles Street) leading towards the Charles
Bridge (Karlův most). On your way, have a
look at **Clam-Gallas Palace** (Clam-Gallasův
palác) at the corner of Husova street,
nowadays the Prague archives, with Matthias
Braun's baroque statues. Further down, on
the right, you will see the **House of the
Golden Well** (U zlaté studně). There is a
legend that at the bottom of the deep well in
this house something seems to glitter: a
treasure? Long ago, a maid who was curious
to discover the answer fell into the well and

*The Charles Bridge
attract thousands of
visitors all through
the year.*

The richly decorated Mirror Hall of the Clementinum makes an atmospheric setting for concerts.

was drowned. At night she still walks the streets with Prague's other ghosts – the executed martyrs from Staroměstské náměstí, the Iron Man and the burning skeleton of a money lender.

On the right side of Karlova, between Seminářská and Křížovnická streets, is the huge complex of baroque buildings of the Jesuit College, **Clementinum** (Klementinum). Today the National Library and Technical Library are housed here. In its **Mirror Hall** (Zrcadlová síň) you can listen to concerts.

Before crossing the Charles Bridge, look at the beautiful little **Knights of the Cross**

Square (Křížovnické náměstí) with the
Church of the Holy Saviour (Kostel sv.
Salvátora) in front of the bridge, and the
domed **Church of St Francis** (Kostel sv.
Františka Serafinského) on your right. A
statue of Charles IV stands in the middle of
the square. On the left side, in the building
of the former bath house (Karlovy lázně),
there is now an arcade called **Salomon's**,
with gift shops and cafés.

   To reach the bridge, go through the **Old
Town Bridge Tower** (Staroměstská mostecká
věž). This was built by the architect of the

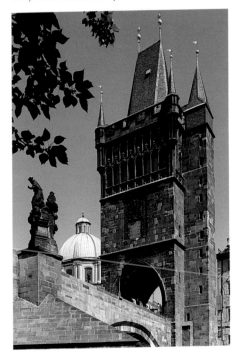

*The Old Town
Bridge Tower is a
magnificent
example of Gothic
architecture.*

The Charles Bridge Statues

Some of the statues are great art, some are not and many of the best are copies of originals in the Lapidarium (*see* p.89). Yet it is interesting to identify the figures.

Start on the Staré Město (Old Town) side, looking across to the castle. Pass under the magnificent Bridge Tower, and the first figure on the left is St Ivo (1), patron saint of lawyers, who receives a libation of beer from law students after their finals. Opposite is the Madonna (2) with a kneeling St Bernard and putti playing irreverently with the dice, cockerel and other features of Christ's Passion. (3) is St Barbara (with Saints Margaret and Elizabeth) whose beautiful hands so entranced Kafka. (4) is the Madonna again, this time in more serious company: theologian St Thomas Aquinas and St Dominic, founder of his own order. (5) is a Pietà. (6) is a Crucifixion at the place where the original bridge adornment – a simple crucifix – stood alone for 200 years. The gold

The Charles Bridge at dusk.

inscription is Hebrew for 'Holy, Holy, Holy Lord'. (7) is Jesus' father, St Joseph, (8) the Christ Child with Mary and St Anne, her mother. (9) is the Jesuit missionary St Francis Xavier supported by enthusiastic converts. (10) is the Greek Saints Cyril (of the alphabet) and Methodius who Christianized the Slavs. (11) is St Christopher, (12) John the Baptist, (13) St Francis Borgia. St Wenceslas, Norbert and Sigismund (14) are much less interesting than the commemorative bronze cross on the right: this is where Saint John Nepomuk was flung to his death. (15) is St Ludmilla with the young

Wenceslas thoughtfully holding the veil which smothered her while (16) is St John Nepomuk himself. (17) is St Francis the Seraphic and (18) St Anthony of Padua. (19) is the legendary figure of Bruncvík. (20) is St Vincent Ferrer with the hermit St Procopius. St Jude Thaddaeus (21) is holding the club which beat his brains out. He is the patron of those in peril, which could be useful because if the lantern behind St Nicholas of Tolentino (22) goes out when you are passing, it is said you will die within the year. St Augustine (23) faces St Luitgard (24), the blind nun and one of the best sculptures on the bridge. St Cajetan (25) St Adalbert (26) and St Philip Benitius (27) are less fun than the founders of the Trinitarian Order (28) who rescued Christian captives (note the Turk and his evil dog). St Vitus (29) may never dance again after the lion's attentions and St Wenceslas (30) has problems of his own, but Saints Cosma and Damian (31) – who tended the sick – might help.

Malá Strana

Charles Bridge

Old Town
(Staré Město)

bridge, **Petr Parléř**. On the façade of the
tower are the medieval statues of Charles IV,
his son Václav IV and of three saints, St
Vitus, patron of the bridge, St Vojtěch and St
Zigmund. The tower was once used as a
prison – on the walls inside you can still see
graffiti etched by prisoners.

A poet once called the Charles Bridge 'a
ring on Prague's hand'. Some people swear
that they have heard the statues on the
bridge talking to one another when all the
tourists have gone. The bridge was built in
the reign of Charles IV, in the 14C, to
replace an older structure called Judith's
Bridge. There is a legend that the builders
of the bridge wanted it to be very durable so
they asked every village around Prague to
send a waggon of eggs to be added to the
mortar. One village, afraid that their eggs
would break, sent them hard boiled.

After crossing the bridge, you could make
a brief detour down the steps to **Kampa
Island** (*see* p.63).

The Royal Route lies straight ahead under
the Bridge Tower, but before going through,
look to the right at the **House of the Three
Ostriches** (U Tří Pštrosů) with its frescoed
façade; then turn back for the beautiful view
of Staré Město's towers and spires.

You have now reached the **Malá Strana**
(the Little Quarter), a picturesque area of
palaces, gardens and narrow streets. Follow
Mostecká until you reach Malostranské
náměstí . This square is divided into a lower
and upper part by the dominating features
of Malá Strana, the **Church of St Nicholas**
(Kostel sv. Mikuláše), with its green copper
cupola, and the former Jesuit College. The
church was built in the first half of the 18C
by **Christoph Diezenhofer** and his son,

*The Church of St
Nicholas, with its
70m (230ft) dome,
is one of the Little
Quarter's best-
known landmarks.*

Palko's The Glory of the Holy Trinity in the dome of the Church of St Nicholas is a masterpiece.

Kilian, Prague's most important and prolific baroque architects. The interior is indeed a *tour de force* . Mozart played the organ here, and the movement and richness of the decoration delight the eye. Look for Palko's fresco of *The Glory of the Holy Trinity* in the cupola, and Krackev's magnificent *Apotheosis of St Nicolas*, the largest painting in Prague.

On the lower square is the former **Town Hall**, as well as the **Kaiserstein Palace** where the opera singer Emmy Destinn lived from

1908 to 1914. On the upper square, in front of the church, is the **Liechtenstein Palace**, formerly the School of Politic Studies of the Communist Party Central Committee. The building now belongs to the Academy of Music and concerts are often held there.

The Royal Route leads up the hill to the castle. Follow busy Nerudova street, named after the Czech writer **Jan Neruda**. He described the life and characters of this quarter in his *Stories from Malá Strana*. Neruda's parents had a shop in this street and the writer himself lived in the house

There are many delightful streets to explore in the Little Quarter.

Brokoff's sculptures of two Moors support the balcony of Morzin Palace, which now houses the Romanian Embassy.

called **At the Two Suns**. Further along look out for the **Morzin Palace**, with its sculptures by Brokoff. The two Moors supporting the balcony are popular amongPrague students because touching their toes is believed to bring luck in exams.

As you climb, look too at the house signs. Before the Empress Maria Theresa decreed that houses had to be numbered, every house was known by the name of its sign. In Nerudova street, look for the Three Violins, the House of the Golden Cup and the House of St John Nepomuk. On your right is the **Thun-Hohenstein Palace** (Thun-Hohenštejnský Palác), now the Italian Embassy. Turn sharp right into Ke Hradu street for Prague Castle, and enjoy the wonderful view of Prague over the rooftops.

PRAGUE CASTLE AND HRADČANY

From the tram stop Pohořelec – Strahov Monastery – Loretánská street – Czernin Palace –The Loreto – Nový Svět – Hradčanské náměstí – Prague Castle (Pražský hrad) – Old Palace Stairs – Malostranská metro station

Take tram no 22 and get off at the **Pohořelec** stop. This large square takes its name, which means 'burnt place', from the terrible fires which destroyed it in 1420, 1541 and 1742.

When you get off the tram, look down the square to the castle. On the upper side, partially hidden behind houses, is the gate to the **Strahov Monastery** (Strahovský Klášter). The gateway was designed by Anselmo Lurago, one of Prague's most important baroque architects. The monastery was founded in 1140 by the Premonstratensian Order, renowned for its scientific work, to whom it has now been returned. The **Strahov Library,** one of the richest in Prague, is well worth a visit. From the garden of the monastery, on the slope of Petřín Hill, there is a wonderful view of Prague and the castle.

Return to Pohořelec and follow Loretánská street down to Loretánské náměstí. Both take their name from **The Loreto** (Loreta), a place of pilgrimage built in the 17C and 18C by the Lobkowicz family to protect a copy of the Santa Casa, or Holy House of the Virgin Mary. According to legend, the house was carried by angels from Nazareth to a village in Italy called Loretto. In the 17C, it was fashionable to build copies of the Santa Casa, and if you enter you can see not only the 'Holy House' but also the **Loreto Treasury** containing

41

many works of art – monstrances, chalices and other religious objects. The most popular is the so-called 'Prague Sun', a silver monstrance (the vessel which contains the host) decorated with 6 222 diamonds. This was made in 1698, based on a drawing by Fischer von Erlach, the Viennese architect. In the **Loreto Tower** there is a set of 27 bells which every hour chime a song of praise to the Virgin Mary.

In Loretánské náměstí, in front of the main entrance to the Loreto, you can see the daunting early Baroque façade of the **Černín Palace** (Černínský palác). Since the first Czechoslovak Republic, the Czech Ministry of Foreign Affairs has had its offices here. After the Second World War Jan Masaryk, the son of T G Masaryk, the first Czechoslovak President, was the Minister of Foreign Affairs and this was his official

The Loreto has been a place of pilgrimage ever since it was first built, in the 17C.

The grandiose Černín Palace was designed by Francesco Caratti, and has a façade some 150m long.

Restoration work in 1971 revealed the cream and brown sgraffito on the front of the Martinic Palace.

residence. A few days after the Communists came to power in February 1948 he was found dead in the courtyard below his bathroom. His death has never been explained.

Leave Loretánské náměstí by Černínská street to find one of the most picturesque streets in Hradčany – the New World (Nový Svět). At the end of Nový Svět, after the Golden Pear restaurant (U zlaté hrušky), turn right and follow Kanovnická street, with its baroque church dedicated to **St John Nepomuk**, until you reach Hradčanské náměstí.

On the corner of Kanovnická street and Hradčanské náměstí is the Renaissance **Martinic Palace** (Martinický palác) which once belonged to the family of a defenestrated governor. To the right, most of the west side of the square is taken up by the baroque façade of the **Tuscany Palace** (Toskánský palác). On the corner of the square at the Radnické steps you can see the small house which was once the Town Hall of Hradčany. On the same side is the Renaissance **Schwarzenberg Palace** (Schwarzenberský palác) with its distinctive *sgraffito*, now the **Military History Museum**. Opposite, next door to the Prague Castle entrance, is the late baroque or rococo **Palace of the Archbishop** (Arcibiskupský palác). To the left of this is the well-hidden entrance to the **Sternberg Palace** (Šternberský palác), now the home of the National Gallery. Here you can see a small but excellent collection of European art.

Before entering **Prague Castle**, you might enjoy a drink in the Kajetánka café which has a wonderful view of the city.

The Palace of the Archbishop has a rococo façade designed by Johann Wirch (1764), although earlier baroque elements are still visible.

The Changing of the Guard outside Prague Castle never fails to draw a crowd of spectators.

Prague Castle (Pražský Hrad)

The main gate of the castle is protected by the two Fighting Giants made by Ignaz Platzer in 1769, and by flesh and blood soldiers of the Castle Guard, dressed in uniforms created in 1990 by Theodor Pištěk, a stage and costume designer. The Changing of the Guard takes place every day at noon.

You are now in the **First,** or **Honour Courtyard**, built by the Empress Maria

The main entrance to Prague Castle is flanked by statues (copies) of the Fighting Giants, by Ignaz Platzer.

Theresa. Ahead is the old entrance to the castle, called **Mathias's Gate**, built in the baroque style by the Emperor Mathias in 1614. Pass through Mathias's Gate into the **Second Courtyard**. If you want to see the **St Vitus Treasury** – a priceless collection of religious paraphernalia – you will find it in the neo-classical Rood Chapel just in front of you.

To get to the **Royal Garden** (Královská zahrada), go to the left, behind the fountain, and leave the castle by the gate which leads to the Powder Bridge (Prašný most). Near this gate is the entrance to the **Castle Gallery** containing those paintings which remain from the rich collection of Emperor Rudolf II.

Near the castle, in the Royal Garden, is the summer palace called the **Belvedere** (Belveder). It was built in the style of the Italian Renaissance by the first Habsburg on the Czech throne, Ferdinand I, for his wife Queen Anne. The architect was Paolo della Stella who worked on the Belvedere from 1538 to 1541, when building was interrupted by a great fire at the castle. The second floor of the Belvedere is the work of the architect Bonifac Wohlmut. In the garden is the **Singing Fountain**, made of bronze in 1564 by Tomáš Jaroš. It is said that if you want to hear all the bells of Prague ringing together, listen to the sound of water falling into the bowls of the fountain. In the Royal Garden there is also a real (indoor) tennis court (Míčovna) built between 1567 and 1569 by Wohlmut and Aostalis, with *sgraffito* plaster drawings representing the Sciences, Virtues and Elements.

You can leave the Second Courtyard by a smaller gate on the west side, close to the gate you entered by. This will lead you to the entrance of the **Spanish Hall** (Spanělský sál), built by Emperor Rudolf II between 1604 and 1606. Concerts are sometimes held here on festive occasions.

St Vitus's Cathedral (Chrám sv. Víta)

Returning to the Second Courtyard, go through the passage in the building which contains the Presidential Office into the **Third Courtyard**. In front of you are the two neo-Gothic towers of **St Vitus's Cathedral**

The Singing Fountain (1564) in front of the Belvedere gets its name from the sound of the water as it hits the bronze bowls.

The south side of the magnificent St Vitus's Cathedral.

(Chrám sv. Víta). There was a Romanesque rotunda and later a basilica on the place where Charles IV had his great cathedral built in the 14C. Its first architect, Matthew of Arras, began the building by following the pattern of the Cathedral of Narbonne in southern France. It was his successor, the 23-year-old genius Petr Parléř from Schwäbrisch Gmunl, who completed the Gothic choir we see today. At the end of the last century and in the first decades of this, the cathedral was finished in the neo-Gothic style and Prague Castle was given a new dominating feature – the two spires which soar above the west façade.

On entering the cathedral, look out for the stained-glass windows. The third from the left was made by Alfons Mucha, and others by eminent Czech painters. The **St Wenceslas Chapel** (Kaple sv. Václava), on the right side of the cathedral, contains the saint's tomb and his statue by Petr Parléř. St Wenceslas (Václav) was a pious prince of the Přemyslid dynasty who was murdered by his brother Boleslav (*see* p.9). Wenceslas was killed on the threshold of a church in the

Left: St Vitus's Cathedral has some beautiful stained-glass windows.

Right: A statue of St Wenceslas in the chapel dedicated to him in St Vitus's Cathedral.

town of Stará Boleslav, and the bronze ring on the door of the chapel is said to be the one he grasped in his death throes. The chapel is decorated with semi-precious stones, including amethysts and jaspers.

Above the St Wenceslas Chapel is the chamber where the **Bohemian Coronation Jewels** are kept. The strongroom is protected by a door with seven locks and there are seven key holders, each of them representing the highest institutions in the country: President of the Republic, Mayor of Prague, the Archbishop, and so on. All must be present for the door to be opened.

In the middle of the cathedral is the white marble tomb of the first Habsburg king, Ferdinand I, with his wife and son. On the right-hand side of the main altar you will see the richly decorated silver **tomb of St John Nepomuk,** made soon after his canonization in 1729. The **Crypt** is the resting place for other Czech kings, including the 'Hussite king' George of Poděbrady, and Charles IV and his four wives. Their portraits – as well as those of the builders of the cathedral and the archbishops of Prague – can be seen in the upper gallery, or triforium.

The choir chapels are the oldest part of the cathedral, built by Matthew of Arras. Note the wooden Art Nouveau crucifix in the neo-Gothic part of the cathedral, before leaving by the main entrance. Turn left here (you are still in the Third Courtyard) to see the Renaissance **statue of St George** fighting an unfortunate dragon and the **Golden Portal** of the cathedral itself. Facing the south side of the cathedral is the balcony from which it is traditional for Czechoslovak (and now Czech) presidents to speak following their election.

Royal Palace (Královský palác)

The first thing you see on entering the **Royal Palace** is **Vladislav Hall** (Vladislavský sál), where presidential elections take place. This vast room, with its rib-vaulting, is built in the late-Gothic style, with distinctive Renaissance

The medieval parliament was held in the Diet Room of the Royal Palace, which also served as the throne room.

St George's Basilica is Prague's finest Romanesque building.

features such as the windows. In the basement are the halls of the Romanesque and Gothic Royal Palaces. Vladislav Hall was used for jousts and tournaments and there is a 'rider's staircase'. Under Rudolf II, the hall became a market for art works. In 1618, when Czech noblemen stormed into the adjoining Chancellery, they threw two governors and a clerk from its window – the second Prague defenestration. Nobody was badly hurt, which some attribute to Divine intervention, others to the presence of a large dung heap under the window.

St George's Basilica (Bazilika sv. Jiří)
On leaving the Old Royal Palace, walk behind the choir of the cathedral into St George's Square. Here is another castle church, **St George's Basilica**, the best preserved and most beautiful Romanesque

building in Prague. Behind the later façade is the honey-coloured building which replaced the original church of 935 after the castle fire of 1142. Inside is the tomb of the Czech patron saint, St Ludmila, grandmother of St Wenceslas.

Next door is the Benedictine **St George's Convent** (Klášter sv Jiří), founded in 973 by Mlada, sister of Boleslav the Pious, and the oldest religious establishment in Bohemia. It houses another part of the National Gallery collection – exceptional Czech Gothic and baroque paintings and sculpture.

St George's Street (Jiřská) behind the convent leads, via an alleyway, into **Golden Lane** (Zlatá ulička). There are many dark legends about this street of Lilliputian cottages: hints of alchemy and the Black Arts. In fact, it gets its name from the

The tiny houses of Golden Lane were originally home to the Castle guards – who must have been rather small!

goldsmiths who once lived there. Castle guards also lived there, although, with ceilings only 1m (3ft) high, they were either very uncomfortable or not very formidable!

At the end of the lane is the entrance to one of the castle's towers, **Dalibor Tower** (Daliborka), a former prison named after its first prisoner, Dalibor. He was so bored that he asked his guard for a violin and learned to play it. The people went to listen to his sad tunes until his execution.

You might like to visit the **Toy Museum** (Muzeum hraček) before leaving the castle, or see if there is a concert in the **Lobkowicz Palace** (Lobkovický palác). Then go down the **Old Castle Stairs** (Staré zámecké schody) to Malostranská metro station.

The Toy Museum, seen on the right, is housed in part of Prague Castle.

MALÁ STRANA –
THE LITTLE QUARTER

Malostranská metro station – Valdštejnská street – Wallenstein Palace and Garden – Ledebour and Palffy Gardens – Tomášská street – Pětikostelní náměstí – Sněmovní street – Malostranské náměstí – Karmelitská street – Petřín Hill – Harantova street – Maltézské náměstí – Velkopřevorské náměstí – Kampa – U lužického semináře street – Malostranská station

Malá Strana – the Little Quarter – is the most picturesque of Prague's historic quarters. Nowadays, artists and embassies occupy the palaces of the old Czech and foreign nobility, in an area immortalized by Jan Neruda in his short stories. This walk will lead you past the many palaces and through the public gardens which are characteristic of this part of town.

Begin the walk at **Malostranská** metro station. You can reach the same point by tram nos 22, 18 or 12. There is a walled garden with a small pool and several copies of baroque sculptures near the station entrance. Go through this garden into Valdštejnská street. General Count **Albrecht von Wallenstein**'s huge, pompous palace on the left side of the street (Valdštejnský palác) was erected after 23 houses, three gardens and a brickworks were demolished. Wallenstein accumulated his enormous wealth after the defeat of the revolt against the Emperor in 1618, having stood with the Habsburgs against the Czech nobility. Today, the Ministry of Culture occupies the palace. There are occasional concerts in the **Great Hall**, held beneath a painting of Wallenstein (depicted as the god Mars) glowering from the ceiling. Behind the palace there is a beautiful Renaissance garden with a magnificent loggia, accessible from Letenská street on the other side. Concerts and plays are performed here, amidst copies of baroque statues looted by Swedish soldiers at the end of the Thirty Years' War in 1648.

In the **Riding School** of the Wallenstein Palace (close to the entrance of the Malostranská metro station) there are art exhibitions organized by the National Gallery.

On the opposite side of Valdštejnská street are several palaces, now mainly used as embassies. All of them have fine gardens on the south slope of the Prague Castle Hill,

The Great Hall of the Wallenstein Palace has a splendid ceiling, complete with a painting of Wallenstein depicted as Mars.

but not all of them are open to the public. However, you can visit the **Palffy** and **Ledebour Palace Gardens** (Palffyovská and Ledeburská zahrada) which have recently been restored and reopened, thanks to the Prague Heritage Fund, an institution founded by President Václav Havel and HRH The Prince of Wales.

Further along Valdštejnská, through a narrow lane on the right-hand side, you can enter a small square called Pětikostelní náměstí. This means the Square of the Five Churches, although there are not, in fact,

The lovely Renaissance gardens of the Wallenstein Palace offer a tranquil retreat from the bustle of the city.

any. The name comes from the owner of one of the square's houses – Fünfkirchen.

From the square turn left into Sněmovní street, named after the building of the Chamber of Deputies (Sněmovna). Cross Thunovská street where the **Thun Palace** (Thunovský palác) is now occupied by the British Embassy.

Continue along Sněmovní street to Malostranské náměstí. Do not climb to the castle here but go straight on to Karmelitská street, with its trams.

You can make a detour here. The first street on the right, Tržiště, with a pub on the corner, Malostranská hospoda, leads to the **Schönborn Palace**, now the American Embassy, and then on to Vlašská (Italian street). In the Middle Ages, this was where the Italian craftsmen and artists lived. Today the former Italian hospital houses the Italian cultural centre. Vlašská leads on to **Petřín Hill** with its large park and other attractions, including a replica of the Eiffel Tower and a Mirror Maze. If you climb the hill, you can return to Karmelitská street by the 1891 **funicular railway** – perhaps after having lunch in the restaurant with one of the best views of Prague, at Nebozízek. After lunch, spare a thought for the builders of the **Hunger Wall** (Hladová zed') on Petřín Hill. This project was conceived by Charles IV, with the aim of creating new jobs and reducing unemployment.

If you continue along Karmelitská you will see, on your right, the baroque **Church of Our Lady Victorious** (Kostel Panny Marie Vítězné). Originally a Lutheran church, it was given to the Carmelites after the Battle of the White Mountain and dedicated to the recent victory. Redesigned in 1636, it is

The panorama across Prague from Petřín Hill is breathtaking.

possibly Prague's first baroque church.
Inside is the miraculous wax statue, *The Holy
Infant of Prague*. This mannikin – with a
luxurious wardrobe which is regularly
changed – was brought to Prague from
Spain in 1555 and given to the church by
Polyxena of Lobkowicz in 1628.

After leaving the church, cross
Karmelitská and go up Harantova street to
get to Maltézské náměstí. On the right is the
Nostitz Palace (Nosticův palác) housing a
concert hall and the Dutch Embassy. On the
left is the Japanese Embassy, in the rococo
Turba Palace. From the open windows of the

building opposite you can often hear music coming from the **Conservatory for the Blind**.

Off Maltézské náměstí, in Lázeňská street, is the **Church of Our Lady Under the Chain** (Kostel Panny Marie pod řetězem). This extraordinary name originates from the legend that claims the old Judith Bridge was closed with a golden chain. It is possible that this is not a legend at all, and that a golden chain really was used. The Knights of Malta

The entrance to the Church of Our Lady Under the Chain is flanked by two solid towers.

were entrusted with defending the bridge
and rewarded with a large parcel of land in
this area of the city.

Nearby is **Grand Priory Square**
(Velkopřevorské náměstí), called after the
Maltese Grand Priory Palace. In front of
this, on the opposite side of the square, you
can see the **Buquoy Palace**, now the French
Embassy. The wall of the **Maltese Garden** has
been painted by fans of John Lennon and is
more commonly known as the John Lennon
Wall. Under the Communist regime
different inscriptions appeared here every
night which the police systematically
covered with white paint.

Leave the square by a small bridge across
the Čertovka (Devil's Brook) from where
you can see, on your left, the old millwheel
and further on, the Charles Bridge.

You are now on **Kampa Island** (Kampa)
and the narrow street in front of the small
bridge leads to the square, Na Kampě, which
used to be a pottery market. There are
several cafés and restaurants here, and you
can walk in Kampa park with its fine view of
Staré Město across the Vltava river.

To complete your walk in Malá Strana,
leave Kampa Square and pass the **House At
The Three Ostriches** to get to U lužického
semináře street. This takes its name from
the seminary for students who came to
Prague from Lusatia, a Slav area in
Germany.

This street leads to another Malá Strana
garden, **Vojan Park** (Vojanovy sady). You can
enter by the gate in the wall on your left.
From here it is only a few metres to
Malostranská metro station, at the end of
the Lusatian Seminary Street.

STARÉ MĚSTO – THE OLD TOWN

From Staroměstská metro station – Rudolfinum –
Kaprova street – Valentinská – Mariánské náměstí –
Husova street – Betlémské náměstí – Náprstkova street
– Stříbrná lane – Na Zábradlí – Anenská street –
Liliová street – Řetězová – Jalovcová street – Jilská
street – Iron door passageway – Michalská street –
Coal Market – Havelská street – Charles University –
Estates Theatre – Železná street – Kamzíkova street –
Celetná street – Štupartská street – Malá Štupartská
street – Masná street – Kozí street – Haštalská street –
Haštalské náměstí – Anežská street – St Agnes
Convent – Řásnovka – Revoluční tram stop

The sumptuous
interior of the
Rudolfinum creates
a wonderful
atmosphere for the
many concerts held
there.

This unusual walk explores the fascinating
maze of streets of Staré Město, the medieval
Old Town of Prague.

Begin the walk at **Staroměstská** metro
station and look westwards across the Vltava
river to the magnificent view of Prague
Castle and Malá Strana. You are standing in
Náměstí Jana Palacha, the square which is
named after **Jan Palach**, the young student
from the philosophy faculty of the university
who burnt himself to death, as a protest
against the occupation of Czechoslovakia by
the armies of the Warsaw pact in August
1968.

From the square you can see three great
buildings. When facing the castle, the
philosophy faculty is behind you, on your
left is the College of Applied Arts, and, on
your right, the **Rudolfinum** which stands on
the banks of the Vltava, in Náměstí Jana
Palacha. Originally designed as a museum,
gallery and concert hall, the building is now
one of Prague's main concert venues and
home of the Czech Philharmonic Orchestra.
The **Dvořák Hall,** a beautiful example of a
neo-Renaissance interior, has recently been
restored to its original glory.

Turn your back on the castle and follow Kaprova street ahead. Take the first turning on the right, Valentinská, which leads to Mariánské náměstí. Here, on the right-hand side, is the entrance to the **Clementinum** (Klementinum) (*see* p.32).

On your left is the **Municipal Library** built in the 1930s and, in front of the Clementinum, the **New Town Hall** (Nová radnice), rebuilt in the 20C. On the façade, you can see allegorical sculptures of virtues such as Modesty, Magnanimity, Force and Perseverance, as well as more unusual figures including Accountancy and Audit! You will also recognize legendary Prague figures such as Rabbi Löw, creator of the Golem (*see* p.78).

In front of the Municipal Library is the wall of a palace garden featuring a fountain

The New Town Hall of the Old Town was built between 1908–11.

with a neo-classical statue representing the Vltava: the people of Prague call her 'Terezka'. Leaving Terezka on your left, follow Husova street, with its shops and cafés. On the left you are unlikely to miss the **Clam-Gallas Palace** (Clam-Gallasův palác) with Matthias Braun's statues of giants supporting the balcony. The artist incorporated a joke: if you stare at one of the giant's loincloths very hard, it turns into the face of a lion.

After the 'lion cloth', cross Karlova which leads from Staroměstské Náměstí to Charles Bridge. Further on, between Jalovcová and Zlatá streets, you will come to the Dominican monastery with the **Church of St Giles** (Kostel sv. Jiljí) on your left, which has high, vaulted ceilings decorated with *trompe l'oeil* frescoes.

Antiquity and tranquillity pervade the Library of the Monastery of St Giles.

On the opposite, right-hand side of Husova street is the famous beer house called **At the Tiger** (U tygra). This was the favourite haunt of the writer Bohumil Hrabal who came here to listen to the 'beer chat', which he transformed into his short stories and novels, though perhaps there are too many tourists for him nowadays. President Clinton, when he visited Prague, was invited by President Havel to have dinner 'At the Tiger'.

Follow Husova until you come to a crossing of several ways where you turn right into **Betlémské náměstí**, with its restored medieval **Bethlehem Chapel** (Betlémská kaple). It was here that Jan Hus preached the sermons which led to his terrible death

The present Bethlehem Chapel is a careful reconstruction of the original chapel in which Jan Hus preached.

at the stake in 1415 and started the Hussite reform movement. On the narrower side of Betlémské náměstí you will see a yellow building, once a brewery, called U Halánků, and now the **Náprstek Museum**. Follow Náprstkova street along the right-hand side of the museum, and take the second turning on the right, Stříbrná. This leads to tiny Anenské náměstí. Here is the **Theatre On the Balustrade** (Divadlo Na zábradlí) where almost all Václav Havel's famous absurd plays had their premières.

Now turn right into Anenská street, crossing Liliová street where the thirsty traveller can have a drink in the pub King George's (U krále Jiřího) and find the narrow lane, Řetězová. In the middle of this lane you will see the **House of the Lords of Kunštát** (Dům pánů z Kunštátu) with its Romanesque cellars. This ancient house once belonged to the family of the 'Hussite' King George of Poděbrady, who governed after the Hussite wars, first as Regent – while the future King Ladislav Posthumous was only a child – and then, after the young king's death, as elected king in 1458.

Řetězová leads back to Husova street. This time, cross over and go up narrow Jalovcová street into Jilská street, behind the Dominican monastery. Turn right and on the left-hand side of the street go through the house called **Iron Door** (Železné dveře), with a restaurant in the passageway. You are now in Michalská street, where you may be tempted by one of several Moravian wine bars. If not – or afterwards – Michalská leads on to a small square called **Coal Market** (Uhelný trh). Surprisingly, there used to be a flower market here, too.

From Coal Market, go left into Havelská

(St Gall Street) with its fruit and vegetable
market. There used to be a St Gall's Town in
this area in the 13C – a commercial suburb
of Staré Město. It has kept its commercial
character right up to the present day. Go
along Havelská which leads into Železná. In
front, on the right, is the neo-classical
Estates Theatre (*see* p.86). From the front
entrance to the theatre, on your left, you can
see the **Carolinum** (Charles University), a
centre of learning since the 14C.

*The Gothic buildings
of the Church of
the Holy Saviour
and the Convent of
St Agnes have been
carefully restored to
their former beauty.*

If you follow Železná to the left it will take
you to Staroměstské náměstí. Instead, go
behind the Carolinum and turn right into
narrow Kamzíkova street which will lead you
to Celetná street. Behind the Týn Church
(*see* p.26) is Štupartská street, which winds
around the building of the medieval
customs office and merchants' hostel, the
Ungelt. On the corner, turn left into Malá
Štupartská, leaving the entrance to the
Ungelt on your left.

On your right is another jewel of baroque
architecture, **St James's Church** (Kostel sv.
Jakuba). The nave, which is Gothic in shape,
is decorated with baroque sculptures and
paintings – a combination found in many
Prague churches. There are three paintings
by **Petr Brandl** here, plus many other
treasures. Look for the tomb of Jan Václav
Vratislav of Mitrovice, built between 1714
and 1716 by the architect who designed the
'Prague Sun' (*see* p.42), Fischer von Erlach.
The tomb is decorated with sculptures by F
M Brokoff: find the figure of Chronos
(Time) with its hourglass. You may be lucky
enough to visit when there is a concert of
classical music being performed. If not,
there is a very good organ in the church.

On leaving St James's turn right into

Malá Štupartská, which leads to Masná. Go
left, and on reaching a crossing of three
streets, choose Kozí – the second from the
right. After a few metres, at a square formed
by the intersection of several streets, turn
right into Haštalská street. This leads to
Haštalské náměstí, with the little baroque
Church of St Castullus (Kostel sv. Haštala) in
the middle. Go along the left side of the
church and turn left into Anežská street.
Ahead is the medieval **Convent of St Agnes**
(Anežský klášter) which now houses part of
the National Gallery Collection of 19C
Czech painting and sculpture. From the
Convent of St Agnes, go down Rásnovka
street to the tram stop at Revoluční.

*A capital in the
Church of the Holy
Saviour.*

JOSEFOV – THE JEWISH TOWN

*Staroměstské náměstí – Pařížská street – Kostečná
street – Dušní street – Široká street – Maiselova street –
Maisel's Synagogue – Červená street – the Old-New
Synagogue – the Old Jewish Cemetery – the Pinkas
Synagogue – the Klausen Synagogue – the
Rudolfinum*

This is a relatively short walk, as the Jewish
town has always been confined as far as
space is concerned.

There was a sizeable Jewish community in
Prague from at least the 10C. In 1190, the
Church decreed that Christians throughout
Europe should avoid physical contact with
Jews, so the idea of the closed community, or
'ghetto', was born, together with the
wearing of pointed hats and yellow badges to
distinguish Jews from their neighbours. In
some respects, Jewish communities were
thankful for the curfew: the gates which
locked them inside the ghetto at nightfall
also kept their enemies out. Nevertheless,
persecution was more or less constant,
occasionally boiling over into a bloody
pogrom when it suited someone to find a
scapegoat. Prague was no exception. In
1389, half the ghetto – 3 000 men, women
and children – were slaughtered. In 1541
Jews were even banished from the town
altogether for a while.

The situation improved, however, and in
1784 the **Emperor Joseph II** opened the
gates of the ghetto for good and the Jews
called their town Josefov in gratitude.

Today, little remains of the old Jewish
town. At the end of the 19C the Prague
council implemented a programme of
redevelopment. Instead of improving the
drainage, water supply and housing
conditions of Josefov, they simply razed it to

Almost all the buildings in Pařížská street have been rebuilt in Art Nouveau or neo-baroque style. The Jewish Town Hall and Old-New Synagogue can be seen in the centre.

the ground. A thousand years of history were destroyed, and the narrow streets were replaced with airy boulevards such as Pařížská třída.

When planning your walk, remember that Saturday is the Sabbath, and therefore closing day in the Jewish town.

Begin the walk on **Staroměstské náměstí** (the Old Town Square), making your way to Pařížská třída on the north side. Before entering Pařížská, look on the wall of the new building next to the **Church of St Nicholas** in Kaprova street on your left. Here

you will find a commemorative plaque with the bust of the Jewish writer Franz Kafka. He was born in a house which used to stand on this site.

The Church of St Nicholas was completed in 1735, although there has been a church on this site since the 12C.

Walking along Pařížská, it is hard to imagine the narrow lanes of the Prague ghetto it replaced. Almost all the houses are built in the Art Nouveau or neo-Baroque style.

Turn right into Kostečná street. There is a

small **photographic gallery** here where you can buy pictures by famous Czech photographers such as Sudek, Drtikol or Funke. At the end of the street turn left into Dušní, which leads to the **Church of the Holy Spirit** (Kostel sv. Ducha) with a Baroque statue of St John Nepomuk by Brokof.

Behind the church is the **Spanish Synagogue** (Španělská Synagóga). The

Before the Holocaust, Prague's Sephardic Jews worshipped in the richly decorated Spanish Synagogue. Unfortunately, it is not open to the public.

The interior of the Maisel Synagogue, built by the Jewish banker and mayor, Mordechai Maisel.

arabesques and Moorish windows of the closed building are a sad reminder of the community of Sephardic Jews which settled in Prague after mass expulsion from Spain in the late 15C. It is closed to the public, being used to store textiles of the State Jewish Museum.

From the Spanish Synagogue turn left into Široká, which leads back to Pařížská. Cross the avenue, continue along Široká street and turn left into Maiselova street, named after the Jewish banker **Mordechai Maisel** (1528–1601) who was mayor of the Jewish town. Maisel lived in the time of the Emperor Rudolf II and regularly lent him money, thus buying peace for his people. Maisel, who died one of the richest men in Europe at the time, was a great benefactor of the Jewish town. The **Maisel Synagogue**, named after him, which you see on your left was one of his gifts. Today it houses part of an exhibition organized by the **State Jewish Museum**.

On leaving the synagogue, retrace your steps towards Široká. Cross over, and, on your right, you will see another building financed by Maisel, the **Jewish Town Hall** (Židovská Radnice). Originally built in the Renaissance style in 1586, the building had rococo features added in 1765 when the clocktower was built. The hands of the clock revolve anti-clockwise over the Hebrew

The façade of the Jewish Town Hall, with its backward-reading clock.

The Golem

Long before Frankenstein's monster was conceived (or rather assembled) a man-made giant stalked the streets of Prague's Jewish ghetto. Made from the mud of the Vltava river, and animated by the unspeakable name of God written on a parchment – the '*shem*' – which was placed in his mouth, this terrifying being was called the Golem.

According to the Talmud – the code of Jewish law – others have created such beings, but it was a scholar, philosopher and writer, Rabbi Löw, who is said to have created Prague's Golem in the late 16C.

There are many different accounts of the Golem's activities in the city. In some he appeared sinister, but generally he used his strength to help the Jews in their continual struggle against persecution.

However, the days of the monster were numbered. Rabbi Löw forgot to let his tireless servant rest on the Sabbath and the Golem rebelled, causing havoc. Rabbi Löw was forced to interrupt the service he was taking in the Old-New Synagogue to tackle the Golem. The fearless rabbi snatched the shem from his creation's mouth. What was made from clay, returned to clay. Hiding the lifeless remains of the Golem in the roof of the Old-New Synagogue, Rabbi Löw then resumed the service where he had left off.

Rabbi Löw died in 1609, at the grand age of 89 years. He was buried in the Old Jewish Cemetery, where his grave is now one of the most frequently visited. You will see piles of little pebbles left on his grave by visitors, as a mark of respect.

Legend or no, to this day the congregation in the Old-New Synagogue repeat the verse of the psalm that Rabbi Löw was reciting when he was interrupted, just as their ancestors were obliged to three centuries ago ...

A film version of the Golem.

figures which are read backwards. Inside the Town Hall is a restaurant and **information centre**.

Round the corner of Červená is the **High Synagogue** (Vysoká synagóga) which has an exhibition of Jewish textiles. Like the Maisel Synagogue, this building was financed by the energetic Maisel.

Also in Červená is the most precious building in Prague's Jewish town – the **Old-New Synagogue** (Staronová synagóga). This wonderful building dates from about 1280 and is one of the oldest Gothic buildings in Prague. It has been used as a place of worship by Prague Jews for more than 700 years. When persecuted during the pogroms, the Jews sought refuge within its walls. Architecturally, the Old-New Synagogue marks the transition from Romanesque to Gothic. The pillar supports are massive and earthbound, but the nave – vaulting upwards on slender octagonal pillars – is pure austere Gothic. An aisle for women was built in the 18C.

This venerable building is also the final resting place of Rabbi Löw's fearful creation, the Golem. The incorrigible Rabbi is also said to have confronted the terrifying Demon of Persecution itself in the synagogue, tearing the parchment list of Prague's Jews from its bloody claws.

After leaving the synagogue, turn right and follow U starého hřbitova. This will take you to an extraordinary place, the **Old Jewish Cemetery** (Starý Židovský hřbitov). Here, because space was so limited in the ghetto in the three centuries up to 1787, more than 20 000 people have their final resting place, in some cases buried up to 12 deep. The forest of 12 000 gravestones,

Right: Rabbi Löw's grave in the Old Jewish Cemetery.

Below: The first sight of the Old Jewish Cemetery is one visitors never forget.

many leaning at crazy angles, bear symbols of the person's tribe or profession: hands raised in blessing for the Cohens, a jug for Levis, scissors for a tailor and so on. Rabbi Löw is here, and Maisel nearby. Many Jewish visitors leave the traditional stone on some of the graves, and scraps of paper with prayers for the dead.

From the cemetery you can enter the **Pinkas Synagogue** (Pinkasova synagóga), founded by Rabbi Pinkas in the 15C. On the wall here are the names of the 77 000 Czech Jews who died in the Holocaust.

In the nearby **Ceremonial House**
(Obřadní síň) there is a moving collection
of art from the Terezín (Theresienstadt)
concentration camp. Also close by is the
Klausen Synagogue (Klausová synagóga).

*The Klausen
Synagogue was built
on the site of
several small Jewish
schools and prayer
houses (klausen).*

THE GOLDEN CROSS

Wenceslas Square (Václavské Náměstí) is the hub of Prague. This is where things happen: the declaration of the first republic in 1918; the confrontation with Soviet tanks in 1968; and, of course, the mass demonstrations of the Velvet Revolution. Across the bottom of the square run Prague's busiest streets, Národní and Na Příkopě, which means 'on the moat' – a reminder of its origins, since this is the dividing line between the Old and New towns. Wenceslas Square, Národní and Na Příkopě together are known as *zlatý kříž*, or the 'golden cross'.

The famous Wenceslas Square, illuminated at night, looking towards the National Museum.

EXPLORING PRAGUE

Wenceslas Square, originally the horse market, was renamed in the 19C during the national revival. The famous equestrian statue of Wenceslas (1912) is surrounded by his fellow Czech patron saints Prokop (Procopius); Anežka (Agnes); Vojtěch (Adalbert) and Ludmila. It was a few metres from the base of this statue that Jan Palach set fire to himself in 1969.

Wenceslas Square is dominated by the **National Museum** (Národní muzeum). Built between 1885 and 1890 by the architect Josef Schulz, this imposing building was designed in the neo-Renaissance style.

Walk down to the square, leaving Wenceslas and the National Museum behind you. On the right, after Opletalova, is the appropriately named **Jalta Hotel,** built in the post-war Stalinist style. Opposite is the gigantic **Lucerna Palace**, partly designed by President Havel's grandfather. Further down on the same side is the Melantrich publishing house, on whose balcony the grandson made his historic appearance during the 1989 Velvet Revolution.

The façade of the Hotel Evropa is pure Art Nouveau.

Across the square is the splendid **Hotel Evropa**, one of the city's most important Art Nouveau shrines, and on the corner of Jindřišská is the insurance office (now the Polish Institute) where Franz Kafka worked. The lower square is called the **Little Bridge** (Můstek), also the name of the metro station. The post-modernist building above the station has a roof-top café with an exciting view of the square. Looking back up the square, to the right, is the famous **Baťa shop**, built for the great patron of Czech avant-garde art, Tomáš Bata, the shoe tycoon. This world-famous monument to functionalism has reverted to its original

The richly decorated staircase of the Živnostenská Bank.

name, Baťa; under the communist regime it was called Dům obuvi, meaning 'shoe house'.

Both Národní and Na Příkopě are bustling shopping streets. In Na Příkopě you will also find the Art Nouveau U Dorflerů at no 7, and the neo-Renaissance Živnostenská Bank, built by O Polívka between 1894 and 1896 as the Land Bank of the Czech Kingdom; the banking hall is richly and imaginatively decorated.

Národní also has many architectural treasures, including the **Ursuline Convent** (Kostel sv. Voršily, 1678)which was returned to the nuns in 1989. At the western end, near the river and facing the National Theatre, is the former legendary Prague café – **Slavia**, where writers, artists, students and actors once met to exchange ideas.

Music in Prague

There are many places in Prague where you can listen to classical music – theatres, concert halls and churches. The **National Theatre** (Národní divadlo) and **State Opera** (Státní opera) each have their opera ensemble and ballet dancers. The National Theatre's second stage is the **Estates Theatre** (Stavovské divadlo). Listening to Mozart here has a special magic because this is where *Don Giovanni* had its première. Mozart is said to have written the overture only hours before the performance began.

The National Theatre building itself was the first and most significant architectural expression of national revival, built between 1868 and 1883 by the best Czech artists of the period. The architects Zítek and Schulz, the sculptors Myslblek, Schnirch and Wagner and the painters Aleš, Hynais and Ženíšek worked with a passion to create a fine building in the neo-Renaissance style.

There are three main concert halls in Prague: the **Smetana Hall** (Smetanova síň) in the **Municipal House** at Náměstí Republiky, the **Dvořák Hall** in the Rudolfinum at Náměstí Jana Palacha and the **Congress Hall** in the Palace of Culture near Vyšehrad. The **Rudolfinum** is the home of the prestigious Czech Philharmonic Orchestra.

In the Municipal House, the first and the last concerts of the Prague Spring Music Festival (Pražské Jaro) are held. This international music festival begins every year on 12 May – the anniversary of Smetana's death – with his cycle of six symphonic poems *My Country* (*Má vlast*). It finishes at the beginning of June with Beethoven's *9th symphony* and *Ode to Joy*.

All the year round there is classical music in halls and churches: the **House of the Stone Bell** at Staroměstské náměstí; **St Nicholas**; **St James's** and **St Simon and St Jude's** churches in the Old Town; the **Nostitz Palace** and **Liechtenstein Palace**; **St**

Prague National Theatre's lavish interior.

Nicholas and **Our Lady Under the Chain** in Malá Strana; the **Lobkowicz Palace**; **St George's Basilica**, and sometimes the **Spanish Hall** at the castle.

For jazz or rock music, look in Prague newspapers, as venues often change. There are several long-established clubs, such as **Reduta** in Národní street; **Agharta Jazz Centrum** in Krakovská street, and the **Metropolitan Jazz Club** in Jungmannova street. There is also an International Jazz Festival in October.

At the **Exhibition Ground** (Výstaviště) in Prague 7, you can listen to recorded music and watch performances combining jets of water and lights at **Křižík's Fountain.**

The Prague Information Services (PIS) has current details on all kinds of music.

The impressive central staircase of the National Museum.

MUSEUMS AND GALLERIES

The National Museum (Národní muzeum)

Prague 1, Václavské náměstí, 68
Open daily 10 – 6; closed every first Tuesday of the month
Permanent exhibitions of mineralogy, palaeontology and zoology. Historical and anthropological exhibitions. Frequent temporary exhibitions. In the **Pantheon**, visitors can see busts and statues of the great personalities of Czech science and art.

The Dvořák Museum (Muzeum Antonína Dvořáka)

Prague 2, Ke Karlovu 20
Open Tuesday to Sunday 10 – 5

Bertramka or **Mozart Museum**

Prague 5, Mozartova 169
Open daily 9.30 – 6

The Lobkowicz Palace (Lobkovický palác)

Prague Castle, Jiřská street
Opens Tuesday to Sunday 9 – 5
This houses another part of the National
Museum's historical exhibition.

The Lapidarium

Prague 7, Výstaviště
Open Tuesday to Friday 12 – 6; Saturday and
Sunday 10 – 12 and 1 – 6
Sculpture including originals of statues from
the Charles Bridge.

*The Dvořák
Museum is housed
in what was once
the Michna
Summer Palace,
later known as Vila
Amerika after a
nearby inn.*

The Smetana Museum (Muzeum Bedřicha Smetany)

Prague 1, Novotného lávka
(Closed for reconstruction)

The Toy Museum (Muzeum hraček)

Prague 1, Prague Castle, Jiřská street

Open daily 9.30 – 5.30
Founded by the Czech collector and painter
Ivan Steiger.

Museum of the City of Prague
(Muzeum hlavního města Prahy)
Prague 8, Na Poříčí 52
Open Tuesday to Sunday 10 – 6
History of the city and its inhabitants.

Museum of Military History
(Vojenské historické muzeum)
Prague 1, Schwarzenberg Palace,
Hradčanské náměstí 2
Open Tuesday to Sunday 10 – 6
Paraphernalia of warfare before 1918.

National Technical Museum
(Národní technické muzeum)
Prague 7, Kostelní 42
Open Tuesday to Sunday 9 – 5
Transport, astronomy, time measurement,
history of photography, metallurgy, mining,
and acoustics.

Museum of Decorative Arts
(Uměleckoprůmyslové muzeum)
Prague 1, 17 listopadu street 2
Open Tuesday to Sunday 10 – 6
European and Czech decorative arts of 16C
to 19C: glass, pottery, china, furniture,
metalwork, textiles, fashion accessories,
books and miniatures.

The National Gallery (Národní galerie)
There are collections at various locations:
(I) Sternberg Palace (Šternberský palác)
Prague 1, Hradčanské Náměstí 15
Open Tuesday to Sunday 10 – 6
European painting by Palma Vecchio, Dürer,

Brueghel, El Greco, Goya, Canaletto, Rembrandt, Rubens.

(II) St George's Convent (Jiřský klášter)
Prague Castle, Jiřské náměstí
Open Tuesday to Sunday 10 – 6
Gothic and baroque Czech paintings and sculptures.

(III) Convent of St Agnes (Anežský klášter)
Prague 1, U milosrdných 17
Open Tuesday to Sunday 10 – 6
19C Czech painting and sculpture.

(IV) Zbraslav Castle (Zámek Zbraslav)
Prague 5
Open Tuesday to Sunday 10 – 6
Contains a small collection of Czech sculpture, but much has been moved to the new Trade's Fair Palace.

(V) Trade's Fair Palace (Veletržní palác)
Prague 7, Dukelských hrdniů 45
Open Tuesday to Sunday 10 – 6; Thursday 10 – 9

1st floor: temporary exhibitions; Czech

Sculptures of artists at work adorn the Museum of Decorative Arts.

sculpture; Action Art of 1960-1980; Cubist work of Otto Gutfreund.

2nd floor: Czech modern art 1960-1995; 19C and 20C French art (formerly housed in the Sternberg Palace), 20C European art.

3rd floor: Czech modern art 1900-1960.

(VI) Golz-Kinský Palace (pálac Golz-Kinských) Prague 1, Staroměstské náměstí 12
Open Tuesday to Sunday 10 – 6
Temporary exhibitions. Purchased by the Kafka society and to become a permanent exhibition to the writer.

The Strahov Monastery Gallery (Strahovská obrazárna)
In the Premonstratensian Monastery, Prague 1, Strahovské nádvoří 1
Open Tuesday to Sunday 9 – 5
Recently-opened collection of old paintings.

This stone bell hangs at the corner of the Gothic House of the Stone Bell.

The House of the Stone Bell (Dům u kamenného zvonu)
Prague 1, Staroměstské náměstí 13

Open Tuesday to Sunday 10 – 6
Temporary exhibitions.

František Bílek's House (Bílkova vila)
Prague 6, Mickiewiczova street
Open Tuesday to Sunday 10 – 6
Exciting sculpture by the Symbolist and Art
Nouveau artist.

Troja Summer Palace (Trojský zámek)
Prague 7, Troja
Open Tuesday to Sunday 10 – 6
Temporary exhibitions; 19C Czech art from
the city collection.

House of Black Mother of God
(Dům u černé Matky Boží)
Prague 1, Celetná 34
Open daily 10–12 and 1 – 6
Temporary exhibitions.

The Prague House of Photography
Husova 23
Open daily, May to September, 11 – 7;
October to April, 11 – 6

The Jewish Museum
(Židovské muzeum) Jáchymova 3
Open Sun to Friday: April to October 9 – 5;
November to March 9 – 4.30
Remains from the ghetto, plus thousands of
Jewish artefacts collected on Hitler's orders.

Prague Castle Riding Hall
(Jízdárna Pražského hradu) and
Wallenstein Palace Riding Hall
(Valdštejnská jízdárna)
Near Malostranská metro station
These two riding halls serve as art galleries,
housing various temporary exhibitions.

EXCURSIONS FROM PRAGUE

Day Trips

For visitors who feel like a day away from the
city, three very different castles lie within
reasonable travelling distance.

Karlštejn Castle (Hrad Karlštejn)

This magnificent medieval castle was built
for Charles IV between 1347–58, probably by
the architects who designed St Vitus's
Cathedral: Matthew of Arras and Petr Parléř.
Karltšejn served as a repository for the
Crown Jewels and important papers, and as a
retreat for the Emperor. Extensively restored
in the 19C by the author of the cathedral
reconstructions, Josef Mocker, there are still
many original Gothic features in the castle.

The **Chapel of the Holy Rood,** decorated
with gold, semi-precious stones, and 129
pictures by Master Theodoric, is one of
Bohemia's great national treasures but is
rarely open to the public.

The castle lies about 30km (19 miles)
south-west of Prague on the bank of the river
Berounka, set among wooded hills.

You can get there by coach with a travel
agency, or on your own, by bus or train,
from Smíchov railway station (Smíchovské
nádraží). In Karlštejn's restaurants, try the
local wine made from grapes grown in the
vineyards on the neighbouring slopes.
Opening times: March and April
9.00am–noon and 1.00–4.00pm; May to
September 8.00am–noon and 1.00–6.00pm;
October to December 9.00am–noon and
1.00–4.00pm.

Near Karlštejn, close to the village of
Koněprusy, are the **Koněprusy Caves**
(Koněpruske jeskyně). They are the largest

in Bohemia, with immense galleries full of
stalactites and stalagmites.

Konopiště Castle (Zámek Konopiště)

This haunting Gothic castle with its baroque
additions was the home of the **Archduke
Ferdinand** (Franz Ferdinand d'Este), whose
assassination at Sarajevo in Bosnia in 1914
precipitated the First World War. The castle
is also a charnel house of animal trophies:
the Archduke shot 171 537 animals and
birds between 1880 and 1906, while Europe
moved irrevocably towards war.

   Konopiště is 40km (25 miles) from
Prague. You can get there by train from the
main railway station (Hlavní nádraží) to
Benešov, and then a short bus ride.
Opening times: April, September and
October, Tuesday to Sunday 9.00am–noon
and 1.00–4.00pm. May to August, Tuesday to
Sunday, 8.00am–noon and 1.00–5.00pm.

Křivoklát Castle (Zámek Křivoklát)

Surrounded by rocky crags and the beautiful
woods of the Křivoklátská nature reserve,
this Gothic castle has a colourful history. It
was a favourite lodge for the Rabelaisian
hunting parties of the Přemyslid kings, and
later Rudolf II imprisoned the English
alchemist Edward Kelley there, who politely
followed the old Bohemian custom of flying
through a window.

   Křivoklát is 45km (28 miles) west of
Prague. The best way to get there is by car,
but there are trains from Smíchov railway
station (Smíchovské nádraží) or buses from
Anděl coach station.
Opening times: April, September and
October, 9.00am–4.00pm. May and August,
8.00am-noon and 1.00–5.00pm.

HALF-DAY TRIPS

Vyšehrad

A trip to Vyšehrad (High Castle) is a journey
into Czech mythology as **Princess Libuše** (*see*
p.8) is said to have had her famous visions
on this site. There are wonderful views of
Prague and Hradčany from the ramparts,
especially at sunset.

Many Czech national figures are buried in
the **Vyšehrad Cemetery** (Vyšehradský
hřbitov), which holds a special place in the
nation's heart. Here are Dvořák, Smetana,
Mucha and countless others. Look for the
Slavín (Pantheon), the giant tomb which

*The twin spires of
the Church of St
Peter and St Paul, at
Vyšehrad, date from
1885.*

commemorates those whom the Czechs count as their true heroes: not soldiers, but artists and intellectuals.

The easiest way to reach Vyšehrad is by metro (Vyšehrad station).

Zbraslav Monastery (Zbraslavský klášter)

Zbraslav, which lies to the south of Prague on the left bank of the Vltava river, is now part of Prague 5, but it used to be a small town separate from the capital. Here Přemysl Otakar II built a hunting lodge which was converted to a Cistercian monastery in the 13C and had great political influence on the Czech kings.

The Zbraslav Monastery houses a small part of the nation's collection of modern sculpture, though most has been moved to the new Trade's Fair Palace.

The monastery was later rebuilt in the baroque style and in 1911 a wealthy industrialist had it restored for his personal use. Today it houses a small part of the National Gallery's excellent collection of modern Czech sculpture.

You can get to Zbraslav by municipal buses from Smíchovské nádraží metro station, or by boat from the Landing Stage (Přístaviště parníků) at Rašínovo nábřeží between Palackého and Železniční bridges.

Opening times: Tuesday to Sunday, 10.00am–6.00pm.

Šárka

This romantic, wooded valley is named after the tragic heroine of the Czech legend which also inspired Smetana's symphonic poem *Šárka*. In the Dark Ages, after the death of Princess Libuše (*see* p.8), the women formed an Amazonian warrior alliance against the men and the beautiful Šárka was tied naked to a tree to lure the knight Ctirad to his death. The plot worked, but Šárka had fallen in love with Ctirad and in her grief flung herself from the cliff top.

To visit the scene of these unhappy events, take tram nos. 20 or 26 to the end of the line, direction Airport. There is a restaurant and a swimming pool and it is also a nice place for a picnic.

Trips for Children

Riverboats are interesting for the different view they give of the city, and a godsend for visitors with sore feet or tired children. The booking office and dock is situated on Rašínovo nábřeží, between the Palackého and Jiráskův bridges. The boats also stop at Holešovice, near the metro station. Two of

the trips are of particular interest to children.

Slapy Dam (Slapská přehadní nádrž)
This is really a day trip (four hours there but nearer two back because of the current) where the views from the boat are the main interest. There is a reservoir behind the dam where swimming and watersports can be enjoyed.

Troja Palace (Trojský Zámek)
The most leisurely way to reach the suburbs is by riverboat. Troja (Troy) takes its name from the Classical gods and Titans petrified on the balustrades of the baroque Summer Palace there. The formal gardens are lovely, and children may like to visit **Prague Zoo** nearby.

The landscaped gardens are an impressive feature of the exuberant Troja Summer Palace.

ENJOYING YOUR VISIT

Weather
The climate in Prague is continental, with large differences between summer and winter temperatures. Summers are usually very hot and dry, often with temperatures over 30°C. In contrast, the winters can be very cold, with temperatures around or below 0°C. Frosts of below -15°C are not unheard of, and it may snow. Although the snow usually only lasts a few days, and rapidly turns to a dirty slush in the city, Prague with a fresh fall of snow is quite beautiful.

The air quality in Prague is rather poor, and asthma sufferers may have problems in winter and late autumn when smog is not uncommon. Spring and autumn, when the weather is mild, are probably the best times to visit the city. Although it may rain at times, the blossoming trees on Petřín Hill in May or their coloured leaves in early autumn are unforgettable sights.

Food and Drink

Food
Czechs say of themselves that one in three is overweight. If this is true, it may have something to do with the Czech diet, which includes rich soups, plenty of meat (often fat), thick sauces, pastry-based side dishes, and generous puddings. A typical Czech meal is also accompanied by a large glass of superb beer. Prague is a paradise for trenchermen, but lighter fare is also widely available.

As with all cities, Prague has restaurants which produce dreary international food for

the unadventurous. However, more and more restaurants are reverting to traditional cuisine and these are the ones to seek out.

The Neo-Classical Estates Theatre where Mozart himself performed.

First Course

As a first course, most Czechs have **soup** (*polévka*). This can be beef broth with vermicelli and egg yolk or with liver

dumplings (*játrové knedlíčky*) which is a
traditional local dish. But thick soups are
more typical of Czech cuisine – goulash soup
(*gulášová polévka*); or soups with beans
(*fazolová*); peas (*hrachová*); lentils (*čočková*)
or cabbage (*zelná*), usually served with a
piece of sausage. You may also like to try
cauliflower soup (*květáková*), but this is
usually prepared at home and less likely to
be found on a menu. Also delicious is the
local onion soup (*cibulová*) and freshwater
fish soup (*rybí*).

Soup is the ideal first course during the
bitter Prague winter, but at other times of
the year visitors may prefer one of the other
typical starters. On the menu you will almost
certainly find ham rolls with whipped cream
and fresh horseradish (*šunka s křenovou
šlehačkou*). Or you can try one of the variety
of 'toasts' heaped with minced meat, cheese,
eggs, ham or sausage, often with hot pepper
(Devil's toast) or garlic.

Main Course

A traditional main course will consist of
roast pork (*vepřová pečeně*), goose (*husa*), or
duck (*kachna*) accompanied by cabbage
(white or red) or sauerkraut (*kysané zelí*) and
dumplings (*knedlíky*). The meat should have
a crusty surface and is almost always fat. Pork
is highly valued and tastes quite different
from its Western European cousins. You may
also be offered smoked pork (*uzené maso*). A
glass of beer is the best accompaniment to
this food, but red wine is also good.
Traditional Czech main courses are the
perfect end to a day's sightseeing or a long
walk in cold weather.

Beef is usually roasted, and served in a
creamy sauce (*svíčková*) with dumplings. In a

good restaurant this will be accompanied by cranberries. A variety of other sauces are served, including dill (*koprová*), horseradish (*křenová*), mushroom (*houbová*) or cucumber (*znojemská*).

The excellent Czech pork makes a juicy and tasty 'Wiener-Schnitzel' *(smažený řízek)*, usually served with potatoes or potato salad. And there is nothing like a glass of cold Pilsner to wash it down.

Vegetarians will enjoy some of the traditional peasant meals. For instance, '*bramboráky*' – potato pancakes with marjoram and garlic.

Dessert
In some restaurants you may be offered fruit dumplings (*ovocné knedlíky*). These are filled with strawberries, apricots, cherries, plums or even blueberries, and are served as a warm pudding (although many Czechs eat them in large quantities as a main course!) Another typical dessert is a pancake with various fillings (*palačinka*).

Christmas
If you are visiting Prague at Christmas, you should try the traditional Czech meal, Carp (*kapr*). You will also find excellent game from the Bohemian forests in some restaurants in the autumn and winter seasons.

Drink
Aperitifs
If you like an aperitif before your meal, try a glass of Becherovka, a herb-based liqueur made in Karlovy Vary (Carlsbad). The normal measure for spirits or liqueurs is 5 cls (large) or 2 cls (small).

Soft Drinks

If you prefer a soft drink, there are a variety of natural mineral waters – including Mattoniho kyselka, Ida or Korunní kyselka, among many others.

Beer

The national drink is beer (*pivo*). This is usually of the lager type and is served chilled, usually in 0.5 lt (large) or 0.3 lt (small) glasses. Pilsner Urquell (Plzeňské) or real Czech Budweiser (Budvar) are world famous, but many others are also worth tasting, such as Branické, Staropramen, Velkopopovické, Krušovické, Radegast or Holešovické to list only the best known. The tavern U Fleků in the New Town has been producing its own dark beer, made with

Beer has been brewed at the U Fleků since 1499.

roasted malt, since 1499.

Wine

Wine lovers can enjoy a large selection of
Moravian wines, and Bohemian wines are
also available. Most wines are white, made
from Muller Thurgau, Traminer, Sauvignon
or Muscat grapes. The production of red
wine is smaller, but look out for the scented
and delicious Frankovka or Vavřinecké from
Moravia, or Ludmila from Bohemia.

Czech wines are normally very young. If
you prefer something which has settled
down, ask for a bottle of '*archivní*' or '*lahvově
zralé*', which means the wine is at least two or
three years old.

Restaurants and Cafés

Restaurants usually specialize in either beer
or wine. More expensive restaurants serve
both, but there the beer is usually bottled. If
you want good draught lager it is better to
go to a pub.

Cafés in Prague had an excellent
reputation during the Austro-Hungarian
empire and in the 1920s and 30s. It was a
long tradition – the first café was recorded
in 1683. Nowadays some of the old-style
large cafés are reappearing but more often
the newly-opened establishments are tiny
bistros.

Czechs usually drink coffee made in the
Turkish style with grounds, but espresso is
also available almost everywhere. There are
a few places, called '*čajovna*', where you can
find a choice of good teas.

In restaurants, tipping is usual. It should
not exceed 5 per cent of the bill unless a
very special service was provided. In the
better and more popular restaurants
booking ahead is advisable.

Shopping

Bohemian **crystal** or **cut glass**, or hand-painted and coloured glass, is sold almost everywhere in the centre of Prague. It is good value and of a quality second to none. If you want something really special, look at Moser's shop in Na Příkopě street. Here you will find not only glass, but also Carlsbad ware (Karlovarský porcelán), made in the West Bohemian spa town.

Garnet jewellery is also typical of Bohemia. The stones are usually set in gilded silver. Prague is famous for its **hats**

Street stalls selling jewellery.

Puppets make charming souvenirs of Prague.

and superb **gloves**. **Compact discs** of music by the great Czech composers make a pleasant souvenir or present.

Wooden toys and puppets are nicely crafted and imaginative. Many puppets represent traditional characters from popular plays such as *Kašpárek and Kalupinka* (the Czech Punch and Judy), *Doctor Faust* and the *Devil and the Dragon*.

There are several good department stores in the centre which offer a choice of goods. Bílá Labut' (Na Poříčí str.), Kotva (Náměstí Republiky), K-Mart (Národní str. – open Sundays), Krone (Václavské náměstí – open Sundays) are worth visiting. While most shops close at 6.00pm, some stay open till 8.00pm or even 10.00pm (*večerka*).

The street markets are interesting to browse around and unusual purchases can be made. Havel Market (in Havelská str.) is good for fruits and vegetables, cheese, flowers, pottery, wooden toys and gifts.

107

Staroměstské náměstí (Old Town Square) has gifts, pottery and puppets, while Náměstí Republiky is noted for clothes and gifts. Karlův most (Charles Bridge) has gifts, pictures, photos, puppets and jewellery.

Entertainment and Nightlife

After many years of silent evenings, Prague now offers visitors a busy street life during warm summer evenings. You can listen to jazz bands on Charles Bridge or at Old Town Square. There is a good range of **classical concerts** in churches and concert halls. The National Theatre (Národní divadlo) plays in the main old building on the embankment and also at the Estates Theatre (Stavovské divadlo). The State Opera (Státní opera) is situated in Washingtonova str. Tickets can be booked in advance from one of the agencies:
Předprodej FOK ☎ 232 2501/2489 3227;
Top Theatre Ticket (Mozart Open Festival) ☎ 2481 1870;

A street jazz band provides lively entertainment for passers-by.

Bohemia Ticket International ☎ **2421 5031**, and at Václavské nám 25; ☎ **2422 7253**.

Jazz is played several clubs in the city including the Agharta Club (Krakovská str. 5), Reduta (Národní str. 20), U staré paní (Michalská str.) and U malého Glenna (Karmelitská str. 23).

The **Black Theatre** offers mime and puppetry, including the famous Laterna Magica, which usually plays in Nová scéna (near the National Theatre).

There are **rock clubs** which attract young visitors to Prague. Some of the better known ones are the Subway (Na příkopě str.), the Bunkr (Lodecká str. 2) and the Rock Café (Národní str.).

Casinos can be found in the larger hotels, such as the Forum, President, Jalta, Palace and the Ambassador. The Queen's Club in Vodičkova str. 25 has a casino, as does the Cultural Palace.

Calendar of Events

January: Europe Festival of Carnival
    Groups
March: Bach Music Festival
April: Reduta – Big Band Festival
Easter Music Festival
April–October: Mozart Open Theatre
May–June: Prague Spring Music Festival
June: International Chamber Music Festival
June–October: Folklore Festival
July: String Festival
    Prague Concert Summer
September: Bedřich Smetana
    Prague Autumn
October: International Jazz Festival
17 November: Anniversary of the Velvet
    Revolution – laying of wreaths

THE BASICS

Before You Go

The Czech Republic has a visa-free arrangement with the UK and Eire, and only a passport valid for at least five months is required. Travellers from Australia, New Zealand and Canada do need a visa, and they should obtain one in their own country. No vaccinations are required.

Getting There

There are daily flights from all over the world to Prague, and the major European and American airlines serve the Czech Republic. Prague (Ruzyně) airport is also a transit point for internal flights to Brno and for flights to Bratislava (capital of the Slovak Republic).

There are rail routes to Prague from many European cities, with international services running direct to Prague from Vienna, Berlin, Frankfurt and Munich as well as other German cities. InterRail cards are valid for travel in the Czech and Slovak Republics, but Eurorail and other train cards are not. An International Student Identity Card (ISIC) provides a reduction on international rail tickets into and out of the Czech Republic.

There are various direct and indirect bus services from European cities to Prague, and details are available from the offices of Čedok (*see* **Tourist Information Offices**).

There are border crossings with Germany, Poland, Austria and the Slovak Republic which are mainly open 24 hours. Drivers from EU countries must have their driving licence, and those from non-EU countries need an international driver's licence. The car's registration documents, the driver's passport, and an international green card insurance document should also be carried.

Arriving

Prague's international airport is at Ruzyně, about 19km (12 miles) from the city centre. Two airport buses run into Prague; one is run by Czech Airlines (CSA) in conjunction with the travel agency Čedok, which leaves the airport four times a day and calls at the main hotels, and the other is a special service run by the airport authority and ČSA, which goes to the airport terminal at Revoluční 25 every half hour from 5.30am–7.00pm. Taxis also offer a fast and reasonably priced service into the city centre.

Czech currency may now be taken freely into and out of Prague, but currently Czech crowns are hard to get hold of in the UK. There are no restrictions on foreign currency, and American dollars and Deutschmarks are welcomed in some establishments. Dollar travellers' cheques are preferred, but sterling ones are also accepted.

Visitors may bring in 2 litres of wine, 1 litre of spirits and 250 cigarettes, and the same quantities may be taken out of the country.

View across to Prague Castle, St Vitus's Cathedral and St Nicholas's Church.

A-Z

Accidents and Breakdowns

All accidents must be reported to the police, either on the emergency telephone number ☎ **158**, or on ☎ **0242 4141**. If involved in an accident without casualties, complete the international self-copying form provided by your insurance company, and keep a copy for yourself. The green card insurance document is ideal for cutting through red tape.

Autoturist provides a network of breakdown and repair services to motorists in trouble, and they can be contacted on the SOS phones along all major roads, or on emergency telephone number ☎ **154**. Breakdown crews are called 'Yellow Angels' because they arrive in yellow Škodas.

Telephone the central dispatch office in Prague for assistance in English or German, on ☎ **2422 2746** or ☎ **2422 4215**. Other 24-hour breakdown services in Prague can be contacted on ☎ **77 3455**, and they can put you in touch with specialist garages which deal exclusively with western makes of car.

Accommodation

New hotels are opening up all the time in Prague, but with the number of visitors ever increasing, especially between March and mid-November, it is advisable to book accommodation in advance. Hotels range from the luxurious to the modest, with a price range to match, and many of the package deals include a room at one of the newer hotels. It is also possible to stay in motels and 'botels' – floating hotels on the Vltava.

If you arrive in Prague without having booked a room, try Pragotur's Office at U Obecního domu, Náměstí Republiky (Republic Square). Pragotur also find accommodation in private homes, which is a fast-growing and often very attractive option, but you must book for a minimum of three nights. Čedok also has an accommodation bureau for private rooms, at Panská ul 5, Prague 1; ☎ **2419 7615** or **2419 7552**.

Students are well catered for in Prague, and cheap student accommodation right across Prague is available from CKM (Youth Travel Bureau), at Žitná 10, Prague 1, open 7.00am–7.00pm, Monday to Saturday in summer, and 9.00am–6.00pm, Monday to Friday in winter. No advance booking is necessary. Young people needing somewhere to stay if they arrive on Sunday could try the Junior Hotel next door at Žitná 12. There are also several campsites within the city and in the surrounding areas (*see* **Camping**).

Airports see **Arriving**

Babysitters see **Children**

Banks
Banks in the city centre are usually open from 8.00am–5.00pm Monday to Friday, with perhaps an hour's lunch break, and 8.30am– 1.00pm on Saturdays, although farther out of the city they may close at 2.00pm on weekdays. Bureaux de change stay open at least until 11.00pm.

Foreign currency may be changed at banks. Travellers'

cheques and Eurocheques are also widely accepted at banks, and credit cards may be used to obtain cash from the larger banks and exchange kiosks.

Breakdowns see **Accidents**

Buses see **Transport**

Camping
There are several campsites within the city of Prague and in the surrounding areas, but they can get very full during the summer months. There are two categories of sites: type A are motor camps with shower and toilet facilities, and sometimes a shop and restaurant, and type B which are basic campsites with toilets.

Two good sites with reasonable facilities are: Caravan, Prague 9-Kbely, Mladoboleslavská 72, ☎ **89 2583**, located in the suburbs; and Caravan Camp TJ Vysoké Školy, Prague 5, Plzeňská, ☎ **52 4714**, on the main road from Plzeň and the border. Čedok offers a complete list of campsites in and around the city.

Before towing a caravan or tent, or driving a motor caravan to the Czech Republic, it would be advisable to contact Čedok in your own country (*see* **Tourist Information Offices**).

Also be aware that replacement gas cylinders or methylated spirit for cookers can be hard to come by, and bring your own.

Car Hire

Booking a hire car from your home country offers the best deal, but the major international car hire agencies all operate from Prague so there is no shortage of choice. British Airways and Czech Airlines, among others, offer fly/drive packages, and there are agency counters at the airport.

Czech car models are cheaper to rent than western ones, and the Škoda offers a much smoother ride than more expensive cars over the many cobbled streets of the Czech Republic. EU visitors will need a full driving licence, which they should have held for at least a year, and the law insists that a passport, a licence, car papers and rental agreement should be kept with drivers at all times.

Children

There are plenty of activities and attractions to keep children entertained in Prague, including a zoo, a funicular railway leading to the Mirror Maze on Petřín Hill,

the puppet theatres, and the funfair. Horse-drawn carriages are fun for visitors of all ages, and there are riverboat cruises as well as rowing boats to hire.

Street entertainment in Old Town Square during the summer months offers a colourful distraction, and if all else fails there are enough McDonald's in Prague to soothe the most fractious of young people.

Children under 10 travel free on public transport; 10–16-year-olds pay half fare on Czech trains.

Babysitting services are not widely available in hotels, but disposable nappies and convenience foods are appearing in more and more shops.

Churches see Religion

Clothing

Prague has a continental climate of long, hot summers and very cold winters, and the appropriate clothing will depend largely on the season. The very warmest clothes are necessary in winter when the temperature often drops well below freezing point, even in the city centre.

Most of Prague is quite informal, although some of the smartest restaurants have a more formal dress code. If in doubt, check in advance, or ask your hotel concierge.

Complaints

Complaints are best made in a calm manner at the time that a problem occurs. If complaining in a hotel or restaurant, ask to speak to the manager.

Consulates

Embassies and consulates can be found at the following addresses:

British Embassy:
Thunovská 14, Prague 1;
☎ **2451 0439** or **2451 0443.**
The embassy also acts on behalf of citizens from Eire, Australia and New Zealand.

US Embassy:
Tržiště 15, Prague 1;
☎ **2451 08471**.

Canadian Embassy:
Mickiewiczova 6, Prague 6;
☎ **2431 1108**.

Crime

Sadly, petty crime is one of the major growth areas in Prague, and many tourists will be the unlucky victims of organised gangs of pickpockets or individual thieves. Trams on tourist routes are particular targets, as are all well-known tourist spots.

The best advice is to be aware of the possibility of crime at all times, carry as little money, and as few credit cards as possible, and leave any valuables in the hotel safe. Never leave your car unlocked, and hide away or remove items of value.

If you have anything stolen, report it immediately to the main police station at Bartolomějská 6, Staré Město, Prague 1; ☎ **2413 1111**, and collect a report to support any insurance claim. The emergency telephone number for police is ☎ **158**.

Keep a copy of passport details and credit card numbers. If your passport is stolen, report it to the Embassy at once.

Changing money on the black market is illegal, and although you might be approached by someone offering to do a deal, resist the temptation.

Currency see **Money**

Customs and Entry Regulations see **Arriving**

Disabled Visitors

This capital city does not offer particularly good access for the disabled, although the situation is slowly improving as awareness increases. Cobbled streets, hilly roads and high steps onto buses all make life more difficult, but some tourist attractions have lifts and others have ramps for wheelchairs. Most of the new hotels have facilities for the disabled, but check what these are before making a booking. It is worth contacting the Czech Association of Persons with Disabilities, Karlínské náměstí 12; ☎ 2421 5915, or the Union of the Disabled, Konviktská; ☎ 2422 7203.

Driving

Having a car in the city centre is not particularly easy thanks to the many one-way systems, parking restrictions, and roads temporarily closed due to building works. It is easy to find yourself in an area confined to public transport and permit holders, and on-the-spot fines are instantly levied. Cars that are towed away can be reclaimed from one of three pounds situated well outside the city.

There are car parks at some hotels, and underground facilities at many department stores.

The countryside around Prague is easily accessible, the roads not at all crowded, by western standards. Roads are

Tourists take a break and watch the world go by at the foot of the Jan Hus Statue, Old Town Square.

excellent and very well maintained, and the cobbles which can still be found in small towns and villages have been deliberately left to slow down the traffic.

If you are planning to drive in and around Prague, bring with you a full driver's licence, the car's registration documents (or rental agreement and car papers), green card insurance, a first aid kit, a red warning triangle and replacement light bulbs. The car should display a national identity sticker. If you plan to drive on motorways you should display a motorway sticker (obtainable at frontiers).

Seatbelts must be worn in the front and rear of the car where fitted, and children under 12 must travel in the back of the car. The penalties for drinking and driving are severe, and no alcohol at all must be consumed before taking the wheel of a car.

Driving is on the right, and on suburban roads you must give way to traffic coming from the right (unless your are clearly on the main road); traffic on roundabouts takes priority. Overtaking trams when passengers are boarding and alighting (except at passenger islands) is forbidden, and trams always

have the right of way so watch out at tram crossings. The speed limits are:

Built-up areas: 60kph (37mph)
Major roads: 90kph (56mph); motorcycles 80kph (49mph)
Motorways: 110kph (68mph); motorcycles 80kph (49mph)

Unleaded petrol (natural and super plus) is increasingly available from petrol stations as more and more western cars enter the country. The sign for lead-free petrol is often shown in German – *bleifrei*. There is a 24-hour filling station in Prague at Argentinská, over Hlávkův Bridge, and another on the Plzeň motorway at the city boundary. Petrol stations are usually open 6.00am–8.00pm. *See also* **Accidents and Breakdowns**

Dry Cleaning *see* **Laundry**

Electric Current
The voltage in Prague is 220V, sockets are two-pinned, and most visitors will need adaptors for their electrical appliances; these are available from electrical shops.

Embassies *see* **Consulates**

Emergencies
In an emergency dial the following numbers:
Police: ☎ 158

Ambulance: ☎ **333**
Doctor: ☎ **155**
Fire Brigade: ☎ **150**
Dentist: ☎ **2422 7663**
Chemist: ☎ **2421 0229**
Car breakdown: ☎ **123** (24-hr emergency road service)

Etiquette

Many Czech people are very keen to make contact with Westerners, and are glad to have an opportunity to improve their English. Remember to shake hands when you meet friends or acquaintances, especially on business trips, as failure to do so is considered to be very bad manners. Do not drape your coat or jacket over a chair in restaurants, bars and theatres as this is considered to be in bad taste; instead make sure to hang it up, or leave it with the cloakroom attendant.

Excursions

Sightseeing tours, trips on the river and coach journeys to castles and historic sights around Prague are among the many excursions offered in Prague. For advance information before your trip, contact the Czech Tourist Centre in your home country.

Literature on what's on in Prague is available at hotel front desks, where you can also get a copy of the various listing newsletters. Watch out, too, for the masses of posters and handbills throughout the city. *See also* **Tourist Information Offices**

Guidebooks *see* Maps

Health

There is a reciprocal arrangement between the British NHS (other nationals should check with their own health department before travelling) and the Czech health service, but in any case tourists receive free medical treatment in an emergency regardless of their nationality.

Czech medical staff are highly qualified, and many doctors speak German or English. If you need to see a doctor, ask at the Fakultní Poliklinika (2nd floor) at Karlovo náměstí 28; ☎ **2491 4824.** There is also a dentist here, and English is spoken; clinic hours are 8.00am–4.15pm. You can also ask your hotel to call an English-speaking doctor.

Private treatment is available at the Diplomatic Health Centre for Foreigners at Na Homolce, Roentgenova 2, Prague 5 – Smíchov. Telephone first on ☎ **5292**

The Charles Bridge, with Prague Castle beyond.

1111 or ☎ **5292 2191** out of hours. There is also a special clinic for foreigners in central Prague at Palackého 5, off Jungmannova near Wenceslas Square.

For minor health problems try the nearest chemist; there is a 24-hour service at Na příkopě 7, Prague 1; ☎ **2421 0229**, and a list of others across the city is shown on chemist doors. Most chemists tend to speak either German or some English, but your hotel should be able to help with any difficulties.

Travel insurance should be taken out as a precaution against accident or medical problems and possible repatriation.

Hours see **Opening Hours**

Information see **Tourist Information Offices**

Language
The Czech language is notoriously difficult to learn and speak, so don't expect to master more than a few simple words during your stay in

yes/no   ano/ne
please/you're welcome   prosím
thank you   děkuji
hello   ahoj
goodbye   na shledanou
good morning   dobré ráno
where?   kde?
when?   kdy?
how much?   kolik?
tea   čaj
coffee   káva
beer   pivo
wine   víno
pub   hospoda
café   kavárna
restaurant   restaurace
wine bar/restaurant   vinný sklep/vinarna

Prague. By far the most commonly spoken foreign language is German, so if you cannot find anyone to speak English some understanding of that language would get you a long way. Anyone in Prague on business would be well advised to learn some German. However, Prague citizens appreciate any efforts you do make with their language. Above are a few simple words and phrases to help you break the ice.

Laundry
Many hotels operate their own laundry service, but coin-operated launderettes are fairly thin on the ground in central Prague. Use a laundry (*prádelna*) or a dry cleaner (*čistírna*) where the service is fast and efficient and the cost reasonable. Some laundries will even do your clothes while you wait.

Lost Property
The main lost property office, the Ztráty a nálezy, is at Karolíny Světlé 5, Prague 9; ☎ 2422 6133. Opening hours are 8.30am–6.00pm.

If you have lost your passport, car papers or other documents, go to Olšanská 2 in the city district of Žižkov, by tram 5 or 9; ☎ 24279543 or 2427 2730. Inform your Embassy immediately if a

passport goes missing
(*see* **Consulates**).

Lost or stolen travellers'
cheques and credit cards
should be reported immediately to the issuing company
with a list of numbers, and the
police should also be
informed.

Maps

Free street plans are available
from tourist information
offices and Chequepoint
Exchange kiosks. The best
maps are produced locally by
Kartografie Prague, and
contain comprehensive, up-to-
date information as well as
public transport routes. There
are also several good guides to
Prague covering the city from
various cultural and sightseeing angles. *See* **Tourist Information Offices**

Medical Care *see* **Health**

Money

The Czech crown (*koruna
česká*) is no longer a restricted
currency, although at present
it is not easy to obtain outside
the country.

Abbreviated to Kč, it is
divided into 100 hellers
(*halérů*) and comes in the
following denominations:
Notes: 20, 50, 100, 200, 500,
1 000, 2 000 and 5 000Kč.

Coins: 1, 2, 5, 10, 20 and 50Kč.
Hellers come in10, 20 and 50
coins.

It is best to take travellers'
cheques in Deutschmarks
(most welcome), dollars or
sterling, and these can be
changed at your hotel, in a
bank, or at one of the many
official exchange bureaux in
the city. Eurocheques are also
widely accepted, and credit
cards can be used both to get
cash from the larger banks and
exchange kiosks, and in several
hotels, restaurants and shops
(*see also* **Banks**).

You might be approached by
black-market money dealers
wanting to buy hard currency,
but these practices are illegal
and should not be indulged in.

Newspapers

There is an excellent weekly
English-language newspaper
printed in Prague, *The Prague
Post*, which comes out fort-
nightly. These newspapers
provide restaurant reviews,
listings and other indispens-
able information, and are
available from news-stands
around the city.

Other newspapers on sale
in Prague include *The
Guardian International*, *The
European*, the *Herald Tribune*,
Time magazine, and the
Financial Times.

Opening Hours

Banks: 8.00am–5.00pm, Monday to Friday, with perhaps an hour for lunch; otherwise 8.00am–noon or 2.00pm. Bureaux de change are open until at least 11.00pm.

Shops: Department stores are open from 8.00am–7.00pm, Monday to Friday, and 8.00/8.30am–1.00pm on Saturday, or all day in some tourist areas. Other shops are open 8.00am–6.00pm, or until midday on Saturday, but there are no hard and fast rules, and some shops close for lunch.

Museums: 10.00am–5.00pm or 6.00pm, Tuesday to Sunday, except the Jewish museum which is closed on Saturday.

Post Offices: 8.30am–6.00pm, Monday to Friday, 8.00am–noon on Saturday. The main Post Office and Poste Restante is at Jindřišská 14, Prague 1; ☎ 2422 8856, or 2422 8588.

Offices: 8.30am–5.00pm, Monday to Friday.

Photography

There are plenty of good developing outlets throughout the city, and print costs are cheaper than in the UK. Film is readily available, although not from chemists; look for shops with signs for Kodak and Agfa, or displaying the word Foto.

International brands of film are more expensive than elsewhere in Europe. There is an excellent film and camera shop in the centre of Celetná.

Police

Czech police wear a navy blue uniform and drive white cars with 'Policie' and a green stripe on the sides. In Prague they are very helpful to visitors, and many on duty in tourist areas speak some foreign languages, with German the most likely to be fluently spoken.

The central police station is at Konviktská 14, Prague 1; ☎ 2413 1111. Emergency telephones can be found at metro stations and in many streets, and the police can be summoned on ☎ 158.

Post Offices

Postage stamps may be bought from hotels (which often also have their own post boxes), and from shops selling stationery, tobacco and postcards, as well as post offices. The main post office at Jindřišská 14 – quite close to Wenceslas Square – is open 24 hours a day, and offers telephone, postal and telegraph services. There is also a *poste restante* service, and a passport must be produced before mail can be collected. *See also* **Opening Hours**

Public Holidays

New Year's Day: 1 January
Easter Monday
Labour Day: 1 May
Day of Liberation from Facism
    8 May
Slavonic Missionnaries Day:
    5 July
Jan Hus's Anniversary: 6 July
National Day: 28 October
Christmas: 25 & 26 December

Public Transport *see* Transport

Religion

The Czech Republic is predominantly a Catholic country, and mass is said (in Czech) every day in all the main churches as well as St Vitus's Cathedral. Times of services may vary, so check notice boards.

Sunday masses are said in English at St Joseph's Church (Josefská), Malá Strana, every Sunday at 10.30am after confession at 10.00am.

Protestant (Hussite) services are held at St Nicholas's Church in the Staroměstské náměstí (the Old Town Square).

Jewish visitors may attend services at the Old-New Synagogue, in Josefov at

8.45pm on Saturdays, but Muslims and other religious groups are not well provided for.

Smoking

Smoking is banned in shops and on public transport, but there are smoking compartments on long-distance trains. In many restaurants and snack bars – but not beer halls – smoking is not allowed between 10.00am–2.00pm. Cigarettes and tobacco are on sale in tabák shops.

Stamps *see* Post Offices

Taxis *see* Transport

Telephones

Modern phone booths that accept telephone cards are to be found throughout the city, with the yellow and black phones only for local calls, and the grey phones available for long-distance calls. Most have instructions in English, or you can get assistance from the English-speaking operator on ☎ 0135. Specially marked phone booths in the city centre show where you can make international calls, which can also be made at the main post offices (see Post Offices), or from your hotel.

For international enquiries,

dial **0149**. The dialling code from Prague to the UK is **0044**, for Eire **00353**, for Australia **0061**, for New Zealand **0064**, and for the US and Canada **001.**

Time Difference
Prague is one hour ahead of GMT, and between March and late September the clocks go on an hour in line with Central European Time (GMT plus 2hrs).

Tipping
Tipping is a part of Czech life, and everyone, from hotel staff to tour guides and lavatory and cloakroom attendants, will expect a gratuity. The general rule is five per cent of the bill in restaurants and taxis, and a few korunas to everyone else who renders you a service.

Toilets
There are clean public toilets in the booking halls of metro stations, and also at many tourist sites in the city. Where there is no entry charge, the attendant should be left a few korunas. It is also quite acceptable to use the toilets in cafés and restaurants. The Czech word for ladies is *Ženy*, and for men's *Muži*. Toilets are marked *WC* or *toalety*.

Tourist Information Offices
The main tourist services in Prague are run by Čedok which has been operating for over 70 years and offers information on any aspect of tourism in the Czech Republic. Contact them for help with booking your holiday, or for a tailor-made trip to suit your personal needs, and they will supply you with a brochure listing all of their services and tours. Helpful information is also available from the Czech Tourist Offices in various countries. In the UK, the Czech Tourist Centre is at 178 Finchley Road, London NW3 6BP; ☎ **0171 794 3263/4**. The Czech Centre, Embassy of the Czech Republic ☎ **0171 243 7981** is a good source of information.

After 1989, many worldwide tour agencies opened offices in Prague, in addition to the state agencies:
Prague Tourist Centre, Rykířská 12 ☎ **2421 2209**;
Thomas Cook, Václavské náměstí 47 ☎ **2422 8658**;
American Express, Václavské náměstí 56 ☎ **2421 5397**;
Adco Travel, Bulovka 19, ☎ **6631 0062**; Kiwi, Jungmannova 23, ☎ **2612 82**; Čedok, Na příkopě 18; ☎ **2419 7111**;

Prague Information Service, Na příkopě 20; ☎ **54 4444**.

Any of these tourist centres will have details of sightseeing tours and excursions, accommodation (including campsites) and entertainment, and also have a supply of decent guide books and maps as well as free maps and street plans.

Tours *see* **Excursions**

Transport
Prague has an enviable public transport system which offers a cheap, efficient and reliable service throughout the city. Trams generally run within the inner city, while buses cover the outer suburbs, and the three lines of the metro wind through both.

Tickets are valid for all three transport systems, but one ticket is required for each part of a journey involving changes (except on the metro), and these can be bought from yellow vending machines at news-stands, tobacconists and metro stations. Children under ten travel free, but you will need an extra ticket for large pieces of luggage. Tickets must

Tram in front of the National Theatre.

be validated by punching them into the machine at the entrance to metro stations, or as you enter a tram or bus.

Travel cards are available for two to seven days, and can be used to explore all of the city, including using the funicular railway up to Petřín Park. These tickets are available from branches of Čedok (*see* **Tourist Information Offices**), from many hotel receptions, and from the headquarters of Prague Municipal Transport Authority at Na Bojišti 5.

The metro runs 5.00am–midnight. Trams run 24 hours a day but at long intervals through the night, and buses run from 5.00am–midnight, with night services every 40 minutes to the suburbs. The Czech railway service is also very efficient and cheap. Reservations are required for the fast through trains, and Prague's main-line railway station is on Wilsonova, near the National Museum.

Taxis operating in the city centre tourist areas have earned a bad reputation for overcharging, and should be avoided. If you must hail one, try to agree a price before setting off. You can get your hotel to order a cab, or call one yourself on: ☎ **35 0320, 34 2410, 2491 1559**, or **2491**

2344. You can also pick one up from taxi ranks outside hotels, stations, and the large department stores.

TV and Radio

There are four television channels which can be received in Prague, the third channel being devoted to western services, including American CNN News and the BBC, as well as a variety of entertainment available 24 hours a day. The remaining channels are in Czech, although some hotels have satellite television which can pick up foreign stations. It is also possible to hear a news bulletin and a tourist service in English on the radio.

Vaccinations see **Before You Go**

Water

The tap water in Prague is safe to drink, but the Czechs drink a lot of sparkling mineral water (*minerálka*).

Youth Hostels see **Accommodation**

INDEX

This index includes entries in
English (where used in the
guide) and in Czech (*italics*).

INDEX